Sad Swashbuckler

Also by Noel B. Gerson

Edict of Nantes
Free and Independent: The Confederation of the
    United States 1781–1789
James Monroe: Hero of American Diplomacy
The Prodigal Genius: The Life and Times of
    Honoré Balzac
The Swamp Fox: Biographical Novel of General
    Francis Marion
The Velvet Glove: A Life of Dolly Madison

Sad Swashbuckler
The Life of William Walker

by Noel B. Gerson

Thomas Nelson Inc., Publishers
Nashville   New York

Library of Congress Cataloging in Publication Data

Gerson, Noel Bertram,
   Sad swashbuckler: The life of William Walker

   Bibliography: p.
   Includes index.
   1. Walker, William, 1824–1860. 2. Nicaragua—
History—Filibuster War, 1855–1860. I. Title.
F1526.27.W3G47   972.85'04'0924 [B]   76-2366
ISBN 0-8407-6483-9

For Margot

Sad Swashbuckler

1

William Walker may be the most improbable hero-villain in the rich history of American eccentrics. No novelist could have invented a more bizarre character. Most of his contemporaries regarded him as implausible. Even Walker himself, after his mad dream was shattered, admitted he wasn't sure whether he had been play-acting.

Walker was a mass of contradictions. He stood only five feet six inches tall and weighed little more than a hundred pounds, yet he wore seven-league boots, and his followers and foes alike thought of him as a giant. He was a shy intellectual who personally hated violence, but his actions were responsible for countless deaths. A quiet introvert totally lacking in military experience, he became a brilliant general and conqueror.

Women found him attractive, but he was so uncomfortable in their presence that he was tongue-tied. Instead, he found his feminine companionship in brothels, though he condemned the practice of prostitution.

Walker had three professional careers, and in each of them he failed. He was a physician who disliked medicine. He was an attorney who delighted in violating the law. And he was a newspaper editor who was so fascinated by his own activities that he ignored the doings of others.

He tried to create his own private empire in the face of staggering odds. At the same time he insisted on increasing those odds; his quixotic nature demanded that he find new windmills to fight. For a short time his success was dazzling, but he came to ultimate ruin because he insisted on making an enemy of one of the wealthiest and most powerful of Americans, Commodore Cornelius Vanderbilt.

Had Walker lived at any other period of American history he might well have led a harmless existence, but the mid-nineteenth century was a time when opportunity beckoned the would-be soldier of fortune. Circumstances made it possible for a romantic to make a bid for glory.

On February 2, 1848, the Mexican War ended with the signing of the Treaty of Guadalupe Hidalgo. The war had been the most frankly imperialistic venture since the founding of our Republic. In it the United States suffered 1,700 dead and 4,000 wounded in battle, and another 11,000 died of disease. The victorious United States also paid the defeated Mexico $15 million in cash. In return Mexico ceded vast territories to her conqueror, including what are now California, Arizona, Nevada, Utah, New Mexico, and parts of Colorado and Wyoming. In addition, the losers gave up their claim to Texas, which had previously won its own independence. As a direct result of the war the United States became a transcontinental power, stretching from the Atlantic to the Pacific.

In 1849 gold was discovered in California, bringing

fortune seekers and adventurers by the thousands to her rivers and hills, and many of them traveled from the Eastern seaboard by way of Panama or Nicaragua. This meant sailing down the Atlantic, crossing overland through Central America, and taking another ship in the Pacific. That is how, for the first time, North Americans became aware of the defenseless former Spanish colonies of Central America, which Mexico was now too weak to protect.

These tropical lands, with their rich soil, unexplored mineral deposits, and mostly undeveloped resources, were populated in the main by descendants of Indians and the soldier-workers Spain had brought there. A few wealthy families of pure Spanish descent owned large plantations, mostly in the coastal regions, and for all practical purposes they ruled the area, establishing puppets in the frequently changing governments they shuffled at will.

A few far-sighted financiers and industrialists in the United States had become aware of the rich potential of Central America and of the vast fortunes that could be made in agriculture and mining. By midcentury men like Commodore Vanderbilt were beginning to exploit the region, paying token wages to the natives and draining off the wealth.

Their callousness, their indifference to the natural rights of the people who lived in Central America created a resentment so deep-rooted that even today there is a strong residue of feeling against the "Yankee." No people wants to be dominated by a powerful neighbor.

At first glance Walker appears to have been an accident of history, but he could have lived and flourished in no other era. He can be understood only when it is realized that he was born in Nashville, and grew up

11

there during an extraordinary period of growth.

In the 1820's and 1830's, when Walker was growing up, Nashville, "the gem of the West," was perhaps the most exciting city in the United States, and her attitudes influenced the nation. No profession took precedence over that of the soldier who fought for the United States, and Nashville's greatest citizen, Major General Andrew Jackson, was both the hero of the War of 1812 and Creek Indian wars and the President of the United States. This great patriot broadened the base of the democratic system of government, and gave Westerners and the common man a sense of participation in the national government.

President Jackson, it must be noted, also established a Tennessee dynasty, with his followers achieving places of influence in both the United States Senate and House of Representatives. One of his "cubs," James K. Polk, also became President, and it was during his administration that the Mexican War was fought. Another, Sam Houston, was governor of Tennessee before a personal tragedy led him to spend several years with the Cherokee Indians. Thereafter, he resumed his remarkable career and led the armies of Texas to victory over Mexico. He became president of the Republic of Texas and thereafter, when Texas joined the Union, served as governor and United States Senator. One of the youngest of Jackson's followers, Andrew Johnson, became President when he succeeded the assassinated Abraham Lincoln.

William Walker was the most unlikely of adventurers, although it is doubtful he himself recognized his limitations. He was the eldest child of James Walker, who had migrated from Scotland, like so many Tennesseans, and of the former Mary Norvell of Kentucky. His two

younger brothers were undistinguished. Norvell Walker is said to have earned his living as a gambler; he also
drank to excess. James, who went into business in Nashville, was regarded as slightly addled by his neighbors.
Only the Walker daughter, Alice, lived a normal, sane
life. She married a man named Richardson and settled
in Kentucky.

William was born in 1824. The exact date is un-
recorded, although it may have been May 8. His father
owned a dry-goods store and was also president of an
insurance company he had founded, so the family was
one of the most prosperous in Nashville. James Walker
built a substantial brick house in the best residential
district of the city; his property consisted of several
acres.

The Bible was James and Mary Walker's only guide,
and the head of the family read passages from it at every
meal. In their house liquor and tobacco were forbidden,
and so was swearing. William, although the brother of
a man who later turned to drink, went through his entire
life without touching alcohol, smoking, or using other
than genteel language. His habits were extraordinary in
an age when many men, particularly in the West, tried
to prove their manliness by behaving in the rough manner commonly accepted on the frontier.

It is fascinating that Walker remained unchanged in
his habits. When he commanded his private armies he
invariably gave strict orders, before entering a town,
that its female inhabitants were to be treated as ladies.
He inflicted severe punishment, including flogging, on
any subordinate who became intoxicated, and when he
caught his brother Norvell in a drunken state, he
immediately reduced him in rank from captain to private.

When he was a boy he was far smaller than his peers, and they, as children will, teased him so unmercifully that he shunned their company. The rough sports of Nashville, which included fist-fighting, wrestling, and a vicious game known as stickball, were not for him. He never went hunting or fishing, and later in life wrote that he had never handled a pistol or rifle in his youth.

He invariably stood first in his class, and he was so precocious that by the age of ten, he knew as much as many of his teachers. His mother, who was sickly, was often confined to her bed, and William's favorite pastime was reading to her. She was partial to the romantic novels of Sir Walter Scott, and it is safe to guess that the puny boy sometimes dreamed of himself as Ivanhoe or Sir Galahad. He read extensively for his own enlightenment and pleasure, and by the age of eleven was familiar with the collected works of Thomas Jefferson, a life of George Washington, and other works on America's past.

The elder Walkers took it for granted that their son would enter the ministry of the Disciples of Christ, but at the age of twelve, when William had absorbed all of the secondary-school education that could be taught in Nashville at the time and was ready for college, he rebelled. His shocked father tried to take a firm stand, but the boy would not be budged.

He very much wanted to obtain a degree, he said, but under no circumstances would he become a clergyman. He further demonstrated his independence by demanding that he be taught how to handle a sword. Every Tennessee gentleman, James Walker included, habitually carried a sword to protect himself from frontier roughnecks, and, the boy argued with unassailable logic, if he was expected to carry a sword, he should

14

also know how to use it as a gentleman should.

His father gave in, and for three years the young man took fencing lessons from a master who conducted his own school. The hidden, ferocious side of William Walker's nature came to the surface only when he had a sword in his hand, He was a canny, deadly fencer who gave no mercy and expected none, and it is obvious that he was compensating for his small size in a world of frontier giants. Even his younger brother towered over him.

He had little time for his avocation, however, at the University of Nashville, which took pride in its standing as the finest institution of higher learning in the West. He was expected to read Ovid and Cicero in Latin. He had to know enough Hebrew to read the Old Testament, and enough Greek to read the New Testament. He took courses in algebra, trigonometry, and calculus. He studied navigation, astronomy, chemistry, geology, and natural history. He took courses in philosophy and, above all, in logic. He was also required to study rhetoric, oratory, law, history, and economics. Theology was a basic subject, even for those who did not intend to go into the ministry.

On Sundays the student body spent almost the entire day in church, where they prayed, sang hymns, and listened to a minimum of two sermons, each of three or four hours' duration. The atmosphere was strict: attendance at bear fights, cockfights, and similar sports was forbidden. Any student caught in the vicinity of Nashville's waterfront brothels was expelled, as were those who attended the theater, a dance, or a horse race. Smoking and drinking were prohibited, and no undergraduate was permitted to own a dog, cat, or horse.

Young Walker apparently found it easy to comply

with the strict regulations and, unlike most of his fellow students, he was never placed on probation. At the age of fourteen he was graduated *summa cum laude*. As class valedictorian, he delivered a commencement address, "The Need for a More Firm Code of Morality."

By the time of his graduation he had decided to become a physician because, as his sister later explained, his mother's ailments had filled him with a determination to aid the suffering of all mankind. James Walker, still disappointed because of his son's refusal to enter the clergy, was more or less satisfied. Medicine, after all, was an honorable profession.

Walker's path was eased by his family's connections and his own brilliant academic record. Dr. Thomas Jennings, the family physician, who had attended the late Mrs. Andrew Jackson and other members of the prominent Donelson clan, found a place in his office for the promising student. There the young man read medical books, assisted in examinations, and listened to private lectures. He spent a year with Dr. Jennings.

In the autumn of 1839, more determined than ever to become a physician, he won admission to the University of Pennsylvania Medical School, which was generally considered to be the best in the United States. There he attended strictly to his studies, showed a tremendous capacity for work, and paid no attention to girls.

By this time he had reached his full height, and he was lost in a crowd. He had dark, straight hair, with a high forehead and narrow face, and his delicate frame was as slender and fragile as that of a young girl. Only his eyes were memorable: they were pale, sometimes described as gray and at other times called blue, and his gaze was so intense that people sometimes seemed hypnotized by his stare—as several of his classmates said, many years later, when he became famous in a field far removed from medicine.

In the early 1840's Philadelphia was still the most sophisticated city in America, although New York had recently surpassed it in population. It had more theaters than any other community in the country, more concerts and lectures were given there than anywhere else, and its libraries boasted twice as many books as did New York's. There were many fine restaurants, taverns, and inns, too, and it was the only city where European travelers felt at home.

The refinements, advantages, and pleasures of Philadelphia were lost on William Walker. He displayed his customary single-minded diligence as a student, had no social life of any kind, and made no real friends. He seemed unaware of the existence of young women, and he was so indifferent to food that he frequently ate bread and tea in his room instead of dining with other guests at his lodging house.

To the surprise of no one who knew him he won a *summa cum laude* degree in medicine in the spring of 1843, after writing a thesis on "the iris," and indicating that he might want to specialize in diseases of the eye. He was nineteen years old, and necessarily must have been one of the youngest physicians in the United States.

A lucrative practice awaited Walker in Nashville, and his proud family hoped he would settle there. Instead, he decided to pursue postgraduate studies at Edinburgh, universally regarded as the best medical school in the Anglo-Saxon world. He must have felt at home in the dour Scottish capital, where pleasures of the flesh were regarded as sinful, although some have suggested that a craving for worldly treats was responsible for the brevity of his stay there—a period of only eight weeks.

On the contrary, Walker felt at ease, but he was bored by the courses in which he had enrolled, and wrote to his father that he knew more about the eye than any of his instructors. This could not have been true, in spite of his brilliance, and is the first known example of the arrogance in all things that he later displayed.

In any event, after spending a scant two months in Edinburgh Walker went on to Paris to attend the Sorbonne. The City of Light, as Paris was known even in 1843, was unlike any place the frontiersman from Nashville had ever seen. Every other building seemed to be a café, a theater, a bookstore, or a brothel. Political enemies met at various salons for civilized discussions. The streets were filled with handsome, beautifully dressed women, and men were gallant as well as suave.

The nineteen-year-old Walker was introduced to sex by a Paris prostitute when a fellow graduate student arranged a rendezvous for him. He was repelled by the experience, later telling his brothers of his disgust, but thereafter he went to brothels whenever he felt the need. Neither then nor at any later time in his life were women really important to him. A grandiose secret dream was already fermenting within him, even though he himself may not have realized it.

Medicine, as it was practiced in Paris, turned him away from his career. He spent thirteen months in France, and his ideals were jarred. The poor received virtually no medical treatment, whereas the wealthy were so pampered that their comfort took precedence over medical necessity, even when their own lives were at stake. Dr. Walker learned little at the Sorbonne other than a working knowledge of the French language.

Still feeling he had to justify his sojourn in Europe,

he traveled on to Heidelberg, which had the best medical school in the German states. The exact length of his stay there is impossible to determine, but he appears to have spent at least six months at the university, mastering German well enough to understand the lectures he attended.

According to a story that cannot be verified, Dr. Walker joined one of the student·societies while at Heidelberg, and indulged in dueling. German students fought with naked blades, and they considered facial scars badges of honor. Walker emerged unscarred and unscathed, so there is no way of knowing whether the stories about his having dueled there have any basis in truth.

The young physician disappeared from history for several months after he left Heidelberg. He may have gone sightseeing in various parts of Europe. According to one legend, for which there is no basis, he went to Stockholm to familiarize himself with the military career of the great King Gustavus II Adolphus. Inasmuch as he had never demonstrated the slightest interest in wars and campaigns, the tale could well be apocryphal.

Walker may have gone to Madrid and Barcelona, but that is not certain either. However, by the end of his stay on the Continent he had picked up the beginnings of a working use of Spanish, and with his usual genius for languages he soon mastered the tongue.

Early in 1845 he showed up in London, a city he loathed and later described as "depraved." No details are available regarding his stay there, so there is no way of knowing what happened to cause his dislike of the glittering British metropolis. From there he returned to Edinburgh to hear some lectures by a professor who had been on leave during his previous visit, and again

19

he was disillusioned, later calling his teacher "an ig-noramus."

Late in the spring of 1845, the twenty-one-year old physician returned to Nashville, where he opened an office.

He was shocked to find his mother permanently bed-ridden and near death from what three physicians diag-nosed as "neuralgia, melancholia, and rheumatism." He examined her himself, and could neither disagree with the diagnosis nor prescribe a cure. His sister Alice is the authority for the statement that his inability to help his dying mother was responsible for turning him away from his profession. In Edinburgh he had listened to lectures by "fools." In Paris he had seen the poor go without treatment and the rich mistreated in accord-ance with their own whims. Now he could do nothing to help the one person on earth for whom he cared.

Medicine, he decided, was no science, but a primitive profession based on tribal myths and superstitions. Mary Norvell Walker died in the autumn of 1845, and a month later her eldest son abandoned the calling to which he had uninterruptedly devoted the previous six years of his life.

2

William Walker's family was stunned when he told them he intended to give up medicine and read for the law, but his decision is relatively easy to understand. He thought of himself as a gentleman, his academic record proved he was an intellectual, and it would not have occurred to him, at twenty-one, to lead any life other than one in an established profession.

He now proposed to go to New Orleans, the largest and most prosperous city in the South. Not only would he find an atmosphere similar to that which he had enjoyed in Paris, but law in Louisiana was based on the Code Napoléon, promulgated in France by Napoleon Bonaparte, and he thought it superior to the American system of jurisprudence.

James Walker balked. He had supported his son throughout his six years of medical study and travel. William's record and his family's standing in Nashville ensured him a solid medical practice and an honored place in local society. It was madness to give up medicine and begin the study of another profession. If William insisted, he would have to do it without any further financial assistance from his father or family friends.

William went, after reading law for a few weeks in the Nashville office of Edward Ewing, a prominent attorney and family friend. He had a natural aptitude for the law, he said, and he paid no attention to his father or the family friends who tried to dissuade him. For the first time he stubbornly refused to listen to anyone.

He had inherited a small sum of money from his mother, barely enough to support him for the two years of study required under Louisiana law to become a member of the bar. Food, clothing, and shelter meant little to him, so he envisaged no problem.

In New Orleans he rented a tiny room, lived on bread and tea, as he had done while attending medical school, and for two years devoured the Code Napoléon. Occasionally, when he could afford it, he visited a prostitute, and through one of these young women he met Edmund Randolph, the clerk of the United States Circuit Court.

Randolph, who was five years Walker's senior, was a grandson of the first Attorney General of the United States, and a bright and prosperous young lawyer who was at home in the best social circles of New Orleans. He became Walker's friend, the only real friend he ever had.

The two were different in every way. Randolph was polished, urbane, well dressed, a practical politician who took a pragmatic approach to the law. Walker was homely, his old-fashioned clothes were several sizes too large for him, and in the presence of people he didn't know he became glum, silent, and withdrawn. Only Randolph realized his friend was endowed with superior intellectual qualities and had an incisive mind, an instinct for logic, and an ability to grasp the legal principles behind the mere facts of a case or argument.

In 1847, when Walker was admitted to the Louisiana bar, he and Randolph went into partnership, opening an office together on Canal Street. The well-connected Randolph encountered no problems. He knew every judge, every prosecutor in the city, and he was not averse to engaging in behind-the-scenes maneuvers if such activities helped him win cases, which they did. Walker was a purist, who insisted on abiding by the spirit and letter of the law. On the infrequent occasions when he appeared in court, however, he showed a surprising talent for addressing judges and juries, speaking with a cogent clarity, and occasionally indulging in flights of soaring rhetoric.

He had few such opportunities because his dour personality made it difficult for him to obtain clients. Most people who came to Randolph and Walker either asked for Randolph or, if he was unavailable, went elsewhere for legal services. Walker had to scrape in order to earn a living, and was able to survive only because Randolph paid him fees to do research and write briefs.

After spending a year as a practicing attorney Walker was as disillusioned with the law as he had been with medicine. Some historians have suggested that he was a perfectionist who soured on medicine and law because, in the practice of either, it was impossible to live up to one's professional ideals. There could be a measure of truth in this theory, but the real reason may have been that Walker, who subsequently revealed himself as a flaming romantic who craved dramatic adventure, was a restless soul who had not yet found the right outlet for his cravings.

By this time it had become urgently important that he make a name for himself and earn a reasonably good

living. Even though he was drifting he had a deep-rooted inner drive that he kept concealed from the world;
he was determined to win fame for himself, to make the
world aware of William Walker.

His situation was compounded because, for the first
and only time in his life, he fell in love.

Through Randolph he met Ellen Galt Martin, a bru-
nette beauty two years younger than he, who lived with
her widowed mother, Clarinda, in a large house in New
Orleans. Ellen's married brothers were prominent
financially and socially.

Ellen had a physical handicap, which she had coura-
geously overcome: she was deaf, and had been since
stricken with scarlet fever as a small child. Some
sources have stated that she was also mute, but no evidence supports such a claim. It is true, however, that
she found it convenient to converse in sign language.
When she attended a ball, which she did frequently, she
carried a gold pencil and a pad of paper so she could
talk with the young men who were attracted to her.

William Walker fell in love with Ellen Martin at first
sight, and she returned the interest of this tiny, clumsy
young man who found social intercourse with most
people painful. He quickly learned sign language, and
soon he was pouring out his innermost thoughts to her.
Ellen shared his idealism, so she encouraged and supported his views.

At some time in 1847, while trying without success to
practice law, Walker asked Mrs. Martin for her daughter's hand. The widow wisely refused until such time as
he could support a wife, but permitted him to continue
calling at their home.

Walker spent every evening with Ellen, both of them
speaking in sign language as rapidly as their fingers

could move. Ellen concurred in Walker's opinions, and she alone knew his innermost ambitions; to her he confided the wish that civilization be transformed into Utopia.

The similarity of their sympathies was remarkable. For example, Walker had grown up in a family opposed to slavery on religious grounds, and he hated the institution, saying that if he could, he would abolish it. This was not a popular view in New Orleans, where the economy was based on slave holdings. The Martin family owned slaves, but Ellen shared Walker's view that they should be freed. They made each other a solemn vow never to own slaves after they were married, and to do everything in their limited power to fight the practice.

Always given to extremes, Walker placed Ellen on a pedestal and kept her there. Years later, Edmund Randolph remarked to close friends that Walker had never kissed Ellen, never as much as held her hand. She was someone to be cherished and protected, perhaps even worshiped.

Walker's financial situation was critical. He desperately wanted to get married, but he had virtually no clients. He thought of returning to medicine, a change he would have made for Ellen's sake, but she wouldn't permit it. Sharing his idealism, she refused to let him do anything contrary to his principles.

In January, 1848, an unexpected opportunity beckoned. Two veteran newspapermen, J. C. McClure and A. H. Hayes, resigned from the staff of the New Orleans *Delta*, intending to publish a rival newspaper of their own, the *Daily Crescent*. Their funds were limited, but they were convinced that if they hired the right people, they would gain a large circulation.

William Walker was one of the people they wanted to

hire, and they offered him, in return for a modest salary, the post of foreign news editor. To their way of thinking he was superbly qualified for the job, even though he had never written a published word. He was both a physician and a lawyer; he had lived in Europe, where he had traveled extensively; and he could speak and write Spanish and French, one or the other of which many in New Orleans still claimed as their first language.

Walker was elated. Not only was he being offered a real salary, with a chance to make a great deal more, but he could also make a reputation for himself as an editor and writer. Equally important, thanks to Ellen's encouragement, he would have a platform on which to express his views of society, which he had previously kept to himself. The arrangement seemed perfect.

So, in February, 1848, Walker dissolved his partnership with Edmund Randolph. Randolph must have been relieved, but he remained Walker's good friend, and to the end of the adventurer's strange life he was the only person to whom Walker would listen. Walker seldom took his friend's good advice, but at least he didn't openly reject the well-meant counsel.

Walker plunged into his third profession with an enthusiasm that had been lacking in his brief careers in medicine and the law. Two other newsmen joined the staff of the *Crescent,* W. F. Wilson and J. C. Larue, but they, like the founding partners, were inundated with problems of printing, circulation, and advertising. Walker, who had no such concerns, not only wrote about foreign affairs but soon began to write editorials, too. Apparently no one edited, corrected, or toned down his efforts.

The first issue of the *Crescent* appeared early in March,

1848, and the twenty-four-year-old Walker, no longer a struggling nobody, at first signed his articles with a modest initial, W. By the end of the month, however, his full name was appearing at the end of his pieces.

From the outset, his courage far exceeded his wisdom. With Ellen's hearty approval he launched a full-scale antislavery campaign and began to write daily editorials attacking the institution and quoting at length from the Abolitionist press of the North. No other issue had ever so completely divided the people of the United States. Emotions on both sides were soaring, and in another thirteen years the Civil War would break out.

Certainly Walker was brave, and not even the most antipathetic of his enemies could deny that he had the courage of his convictions. He was also foolhardy and shortsighted. The *Delta* had a conservative Southern readership, and the publishers of the *Daily Crescent* aimed to appeal to that same market, if possible wooing away readers and advertisers from its well-established rival. Nothing could have appealed less to slaveholding plantation owners, shipyard operators, merchants, and financiers than a vitriolic daily assault on an institution that buttressed their economic standing in society. The *Daily Crescent* found it difficult to obtain readers and carried virtually no advertising.

The undaunted Walker continued his attacks.

Even more fascinating is the editorial position that Walker took on another controversial issue. After the war with Mexico a movement of considerable popularity was afoot in the United States to win Cuba her independence from Spain and, ultimately, admit her to the Union as a state. This campaign was supported in the South, where it was assumed Cuba would become a slave-holding state, and was opposed in the North for the very same reason, and with just as much feeling.

A native of Venezuela, Narciso López, an adventurer known in mid-nineteenth century parlance as a filibuster, conceived the idea of leading an army to Cuba and helping to free the natives. He was joined in his efforts by General John A. Quitman, a Mississippian who had fought for the independence of Texas, who had later led a brigade in the Mexican War, and served several terms in the United States House of Representatives.

No secret was made of their preparations for invading Cuba, and Walker—himself destined to become the most renowned filibuster in American history—was outraged. Condemning the proposed invasion in strong language, he called Quitman and López "dangerous and cursed men who violate every rule of law, every canon of civilization, every moral scruple."

The invasion of Cuba, if carried out, would be unconstitutional, he said. It would break federal and state laws, and would violate the principles of reason on which society depended. Civilization would be retarded, and the law of the jungle would replace the very foundations on which the United States rested. A great nation would degenerate and would be shamed in the eyes of the whole world. In order to prevent this terrible catastrophe, Walker argued, Quitman and López should be taken into custody and placed on trial in the federal courts. They should be sent to prison until they were too old and feeble to carry out their nefarious schemes.

The *Daily Crescent* had so few readers that, when Walker subsequently engaged in his own daring invasions of Central America, few people recalled what he had written about the proposed attack on the Spaniards in Cuba. Edmund Randolph must have remembered the strongly worded editorials his friend had written in his righteous days, but out of friendship he refrained from calling this irony to the attention of the American public.

Ellen Martin, to be sure, applauded Walker's sentiments, and thoughts of her betrothed as a lone knight doing battle against a powerful foe. She would have been pained, as would Walker himself, had either of them realized that virtually no one paid any heed to his editorials.

But Walker's inability to influence public opinion to any appreciable extent cannot be regarded as a failure. On the contrary, his association with the *Crescent* was the most important of his life up to that time. Until then he had been a perpetual student, a man who kept his views, if any, to himself.

Now, at last, he not only had a forum, but the girl he loved continually encouraged him to express his opinions. It soon developed, as he overcame his shyness and actually began to enjoy himself, that he had thoughts on many subjects. In fact, the work he did for the newspaper gives us today a clearer portrait of the whole man.

Certainly the *Daily Crescent* did wonders for Walker's hitherto submerged ego. Totally lacking experience when he took the job, he soon developed into the newspaper's star writer. His pieces were pungent, clearly written, and sharp. His arguments were forceful, his logic impeccable. His progress was rapid, and whatever following the *Daily Crescent* developed was due in large part to his efforts.

Only one other member of the staff had anything of a readership of his own. A journeyman printer named Walt Whitman wrote occasional colorful pieces about New Orleans life. Nonpolitical in nature, they stressed what later came to be known as the "human interest" side of the news, and the discerning reader could see hints of the talent that would make Whitman one of the greatest American poets.

William Walker cared little for either of the major political parties of the day. He was mildly scornful of both the Whigs and the Democrats and criticized them in satiric terms. He was fascinated by the revolutions of 1848 that were sweeping across Europe, and warmly supported the rebels in many countries who were seeking improved working conditions for the working man and at least a measure of personal liberty for the individual. Perhaps his greatest hero was Louis Kossuth, a Hungarian patriot who gained worldwide fame during the 1840's. Like many of Kossuth's admirers in the United States, Walker soon was wearing a broad-brimmed hat of brushed felt similar to Kossuth's.

He was also one of the first writers in the South to advocate equal rights for women, and in several editorials he said it was absurd to deny them the vote and the right to own property. The women of New Orleans applauded these views, but their husbands dismissed him as an eccentric.

In one editorial, written in September, 1848, Walker came close to enunciating his own personal creed when he wrote that the staff of the *Daily Crescent* was willing "to lay ourselves open to the accusation of radicalism, jacobinism, agrarianism and other hard names." In the same piece he attacked "the well-fed and the well-clad" for their refusal to concede "that the poor man has rights which it is his duty to assert by all the means in his power—by reason or by force." Had the prosperous gentry of New Orleans paid serious attention to these assertions they would have regarded Walker as dangerously radical, and a definite threat to their existence.

Walker had attained sufficient recognition, however, to be invited to deliver the commencement address, in October, 1848, at his own school, the University of Nashville. In that talk he avoided politics, but confined himself instead to intellectual subject matter. He called his address "The Unity of Art," and it is noteworthy principally because of the admiration he expressed for Lord Byron, the romantic poet who had become a man of action and died while helping the people of Greece seek their independence in their war with the Ottoman Empire.

By far the most important of Walker's views developed in connection with events taking place in Central America, particularly a long strip along the Atlantic coast of Nicaragua colorfully known as the Mosquito Coast. In order to understand the situation there it is necessary to go back more than a hundred years in the history of the region.

Virtually all of Central America had been a Spanish colony, but the rule of Madrid had become increasingly lax by the middle of the eighteenth century. By the time of the American Revolution the hold of Spain on Central America had almost ceased to exist, with large plantation owners making laws to suit themselves and ruling the poverty-stricken, illiterate masses for their own benefit. The poor had exchanged one overbearing master for another, but scarcely knew the difference.

The establishment of independence was completed under the influence of Simón Bolívar, who liberated much of South America from Spanish rule. The Republic of New Granada, which later called itself Colombia, kept the area later known as Panama as a province, but a number of sovereign, independent states were established throughout the region. They formed what they called the Central American Union (or Federation) for their mutual benefit and protection. Unfortunately they quarreled over so many matters, including territorial boundaries, that the Union existed only in name.

Power abhors a vacuum, and no nation knew it better than Great Britain, which seized a portion of the Mosquito Coast and renamed it British Honduras, with the city of Belize as its capital. When Nicaragua protested, the British set up a puppet native government and retired to the background to govern their territory unobtrusively.

A crisis erupted in 1838, when the Central American Union finally fell apart. The British, who had been waiting patiently, extended their rule to the north and the south, expanding the borders of British Honduras, and ignoring the protests of both Nicaragua and Costa Rica.

In 1847 Nicaragua made a halfhearted effort to drive out the British, and London responded, early in 1848, by sending to the area a joint military-naval expedition that cowed the Nicaraguans and forced them to sue for peace.

The United States was interested in these developments in her backyard for two reasons. First, the acquisition of California, and later the gold rush of 1849, caused her to seek a sea route to implement overland travel between the Atlantic and Pacific, and spurred Washington to sign a treaty with New Granada whereby a railroad would be built by Americans across the narrow Isthmus of Panama. An alternate route suggested itself across the narrow southern portion of Nicaragua. Americans did not want this vital link to the West to be controlled by the British.

Equally important was the matter of national pride. Under the Monroe Doctrine the nations of Europe were warned that the United States would not tolerate their interference in the Western Hemisphere. But the British were flouting this basic keystone of American foreign policy by their expansionary activities on the Mosquito Coast.

President Polk's Secretary of State, James Buchanan, openly admitted that the Monroe Doctrine was being violated, but displaying the same timidity he would demonstrate a decade later as President on the eve of the Civil War, he took no firm stand. Many Americans hoped that President-elect Zachary Taylor, who would be inaugurated on March 5, 1849, would order the British to get out of Central America.

In the autumn of 1848, speeches were made in both the Senate and House about the inviolability of the Monroe Doctrine, and many newspaper editorials were written on the subject. None took a stronger stand than the New Orleans *Daily Crescent.*

It has already been noted that William Walker disliked England. His editorials in the *Daily Crescent* became increasingly virulent, and he grew hysterical. "If necessary, we must declare war on Great Britain and drive her out of Central America by force of arms," he wrote. "American interests have been placed in jeopardy, American honor has been stained, and this intolerable situation cannot be permitted to continue."

If no other means were available, he declared, "American citizens must band together as volunteers, take the law into their own hands and disperse the British by force of arms." Here was Walker's first open suggestion that private American citizens take the very action he had condemned in his attacks on the

33

proposed invasion of Cuba only a few months ago!

Soon after President Taylor took office, Walker's hysteria reached a peak. "If the war must come," he wrote in the *Daily Crescent*, "then let it come! America will be found fighting where she has always been morally—at the head of the column of Progress and Democracy."

Although William Walker didn't know it, another American was taking a more practical, less belligerent, view of the situation. Commodore Cornelius Vanderbilt, a financier and railroad builder, conceived the idea of building a canal across the narrows of Nicaragua that would link the Atlantic and Pacific. Being a supreme pragmatist, he sought the active support of the Taylor administration for his project, and sent an emissary to London to enlist the cooperation of the British government. At the same time he began to buy large tracts of land in Nicaragua, reasoning that by the time the political dust settled he would be in control of the property itself.

Walker's anti-British campaign increased the circulation of the *Daily Crescent* and Walker's own popularity as a writer. In March, 1849, he received an important promotion and became one of the copublishers, or managers of the paper. For the first time in his life he had succeeded in a venture, and his future seemed ensured.

Early in the year a yellow fever epidemic swept through New Orleans, one of a number of such plagues that periodically decimated the population of the city. Each day the newspapers printed long lists of the dead.

Walker paid no attention to the epidemic, took no precautions himself, and urged none on Ellen Martin— a strangely lax attitude in a man who held a doctor of medicine degree and had done two years of postgraduate work in the field as well. This carelessness, if that

34

was what it was, came about as a direct result of his preoccupation with his work. After floundering for years, he was creating a solid reputation for himself and was on the verge of achieving financial success. Mrs. Martin indicated to him that if he continued to make progress, she would not stand in the way of an autumn wedding.

Late in March, 1849, Ellen Martin was stricken with yellow fever. The irony of the attack was that the epidemic was waning, and few people were falling victim to the disease.

The family physician was called in, and a horrified, benumbed Walker assisted him. It was virtually impossible to obtain the services of nurses to attend yellow-fever victims because they were afraid they, too, would become ill. So Walker took an unofficial leave of absence from his job in order to devote his full time and attention to Ellen.

For three weeks he did not leave her bedside, and throughout this entire time he blamed himself for not having taken sufficient precautions to protect her. His attitude was unreasonable, since no one at that time understood either the cause of yellow fever or its cure. Nevertheless, his guilt was overwhelming.

In mid-April Ellen died, and Walker was overcome with grief.

Her passing marked the single most important turning point in his life. If she had survived and married him, he might have become a successful newspaper editor and publisher, a man who led a quiet family life. Instead he went on to his unique destiny.

In the weeks following Ellen's death Walker was inconsolable. He returned to work, writing vicious editorials attacking every institution that New Orleans held sacred or important. He seemed utterly determined to ruin himself and the *Daily Crescent,* and in the former he succeeded.

The publishers found it impossible to keep him on the staff, and he had no desire to stay. New Orleans would always remind him of the one girl he had ever loved, and he wanted to leave. So one day in the summer of 1849, the grieving William Walker departed from New Orleans. He bade farewell to no one and left no forwarding address.

3

The ten months between August, 1849, and June, 1850, make up a lost period in the life of William Walker. His father, brothers, and sister had no idea what had become of him, and his few friends and acquaintances heard nothing from him. For all practical purposes he had vanished from the face of the earth.

Then, in the late spring of 1850, he suddenly appeared in San Francisco. His clothes were threadbare, his battered Kossuth hat rode defiantly on the back of his head, and he was heavily tanned, suggesting that he had spent a great deal of his time in the open. He carried a sword, a common accessory in the South, but a novelty in the West, where few gentlemen had yet settled. In his belt was a pistol, the first firearm he had ever owned, and to this day no one knows whether he wore it as a symbol in a land of violence or whether he had actually learned to use it.

Certainly the time of his mourning for Ellen Martin had changed him, and at the age of twenty-six he had been transformed from a boy into a man. His face was lined and his thin lips were set in a straight line; his

37

hairline had receded and his face looked gaunt. Only his eyes, cold and gray, were unchanged, and there was a hint of menace in them. He might be very short and painfully thin, but no one in San Francisco elected to quarrel with him. Many who met him during this time indicated that he resembled a wild animal, ready to spring at the first insult, either real or fancied.

The San Francisco of 1850 may have been the most savage boom town in the United States. The gold rush of the previous year had brought roughneck adventurers by the tens of thousands into the area, and now that land claims had been staked and the region was beginning to settle down, the unfortunates who had not found gold—and they were in the overwhelming majority—were seeking work.

The respectable citizens of stature who were going into business and building substantial houses for themselves and their families were influential, but they were in a distinct minority. Most of the newcomers were capable only of performing manual labor, and they spent what little they earned on liquor, gambling, and women. Entire blocks were lined with saloons, card-playing establishments, and houses of prostitution. Two or three people were killed in fights or robberies daily, and few of the murderers were brought to justice. The courts could not handle the load, and there were too few policemen to protect the law-abiding.

As a consequence, the respectable citizens formed vigilante groups and took the law into their own hands, often committing crimes as violent and senseless as those they were trying to prevent. Human life was cheap, and living conditions were chaotic.

Even at this disorganized time in her explosive development, however, San Francisco was displaying signs of the civilized patina that would make her one of the world's most sophisticated cities. Among the many indications of her advancing state was the craving of her citizens for word of what was happening in the world, and in 1850 she boasted eleven newspapers. This figure is astonishing when it is realized that newsprint, ink, and presses had to be carried all the way from the Eastern seaboard.

One of the more energetic of the newspapers was the *Herald*, owned and edited by a young reformer, John Nugent, who had an almost pathological hatred of lies, double-dealing, and chicanery. The *Herald's* style was blunt, uncompromising, and hard-hitting, and was so successful that Nugent badly needed help.

The penniless William Walker was given a position at once. Nugent knew of his work on the New Orleans *Daily Crescent* by reputation, and he also happened to be a friend of Edmund Randolph, so Walker was hired the very day he appeared.

After work each day Walker wandered around the city, perhaps because he had nothing better to occupy his time, and he was horrified by the violence and corruption he saw on every side. Criminal gangs were running San Francisco, he decided, because they were supported by judges and police officials who accepted bribes.

By the early autumn of 1850 he was ready to launch an anti-crime crusade, and Nugent granted him the right to do as he pleased. His first editorial was a strong assault on the California Supreme Court at Sacramento, which he condemned as "stupid, unprincipled and corrupt." Little could be expected of the lower courts, he declared, if the state's highest court was a laughingstock that mocked justice.

The justices replied through the Sacramento City Council, and Walker went into high gear. Each day he printed lists of crimes that went unpunished, even when the perpetrators were known. Each day he discussed, in detail, miscarriages of justice that demonstrated the inefficiency and corruption of the judges and the police.

One of the most inept members of the bench in San Francisco was the chief judge of the state district court, Levi Parsons, and by the end of 1850 Walker was devoting long articles to his blunders. These attacks might have been forgotten had Judge Parsons not made a serious error: he issued a strong condemnation of the *Herald* from the bench, calling it a dangerous public nuisance and insisting that something be done to curb its activities.

Walker immediately doubled the fury of his attacks.

Judge Parsons personally appeared before the county grand jury to urge the indictment of the *Herald* 's publisher and editors, but the grand jury refused to act.

Walker responded by accusing Parsons, in so many words, of assisting criminals to escape justice. He was guilty of "judicial madness," Walker said, and added that "the courts cannot be reduced much lower than they have reduced themselves."

This was too much for the members of the bench, who held a meeting and offered Judge Parsons their support. Thus fortified, he took direct action and ordered William Walker's arrest on a charge of contempt of court.

Edmund Randolph had arrived in San Francisco a short time earlier, and he acted as his friend's defense attorney. The trial itself was ludicrous, with the judge and the defense attorney exchanging such withering

40

insults that the spectators expected them to fight a duel. The confrontation was avoided only when Judge Parsons repeatedly backed down.

He had the last word, however, because he found William Walker guilty of contempt and ordered him to pay a fine of $500.

Walker flatly refused.

The court ordered him imprisoned and held there until the fine was paid. He was escorted to jail by the sheriff and two deputies.

That same day a crowd of four thousand men gathered outside the courthouse. Most were armed, and all were in an ugly mood. When it was proposed that Walker be freed by force and Judge Parsons lynched, the mob roared its approval.

Edmund Randolph made his way to the front of the crowd, and announced that William Walker was opposed to vigilante action. A basic principle was at stake, and he didn't want to be set free by force.

The mob grumbled, but those who kept their heads realized that Walker was right and that all semblance of order would be destroyed if the crowd marched on the jail. The men agreed to do nothing for the time being.

Citizens' committees were formed to impeach Judge Parsons. The other San Francisco newspapers devoted columns to the affair each day, and Randolph appealed to another court to set his friend free on a writ of habeas corpus. Walker, who was thoroughly enjoying the controversy, contributed to the uproar himself by writing a daily article from his cell for the *Herald.* His attacks on Judge Parsons became even more virulent.

The case attracted attention throughout the state, and eleven members of the legislature introduced a joint bill in that body to force the impeachment of the chief judge. Scores of citizens offered to pay Walker's fine, but he refused, writing in the *Herald* that the principle at stake was more important than his personal freedom. Obviously he loved being in the limelight.

Each day crowds gathered in front of the courthouse and the adjoining jail, and each day they grew more menacing. The sheriff's deputies and the police refused to guard the prisoner for fear they would be lynched by a mob. The rule of law was preserved only because Walker himself managed to pry open the window of his cell, and to deliver an impassioned speech to the crowd from behind the bars. Other than his commencement addresses at the University of Nashville, it is the only address he is known to have delivered.

According to the accounts of the newspapers he spoke clearly and forcefully. Under no circumstances did he want his good friends to tear down the jail and set him free, he said. "I rely on American justice," he shouted, "and the right will prevail!"

It was apparent to all thinking men that violence would break out at any time. The embattled Judge Parsons refused to rescind his order, but his colleagues were more sensible, and after ten days of imprisonment William Walker was freed on a writ of habeas corpus.

Men of every political persuasion hailed his victory and regarded him as a hero. He wrote a glowing article, thanking Randolph and others who had worked on his behalf. The circulation of the *Herald* doubled, and the paper was inundated with so much advertising that it had to increase the size of its pages.

But the basic situation in San Francisco remained unchanged. Violent crimes were committed daily and the criminals went unpunished. The courts and the police continued to accept bribes from the gangs that ran the city, and respectable citizens were still frustrated in their efforts to establish a true rule of law.

In May, 1851, a mysterious fire broke out in the printing plant of the *Herald* and destroyed it. Thanks to the help and generous cooperation of San Francisco's other newspapers, the *Herald* appeared the following day. On the front page was an editorial, signed by Walker, charging that underworld forces associated with certain members of the bench were trying to intimidate the paper. "We will not be frightened or silenced," he wrote.

New presses were ordered from New York, and the construction of a new plant was begun. Meanwhile the *Herald* continued to use borrowed equipment. Less than a month after the first fire, another broke out in the new plant, destroying it and the offices and shops of many of the newspaper's major advertisers.

This act of terrorism was too much for the decent citizens of San Francisco, who formed the first Committee of Public Safety and began to put their civic house in order through vigilante action. Walker, who had formerly opposed such activities, now supported them in print. There was no other way, he said, that the basic rights of citizens could be ensured and preserved.

His enemies now sought another way to silence him. One of Judge Parsons' closest associates was a man named Graham Hicks, a deadly pistol shot who had killed four men in duels. Claiming that Walker had insulted some of his close friends, he challenged the editor to a duel.

Under the code of honor there was no way Walker could refuse, so one morning before dawn he rode off, accompanied by Randolph as his second, to a secluded spot at the far end of San Francisco Bay. Randolph is the authority for what happened.

Dueling was now contrary to William Walker's personal creed, so he deliberately fired a bullet into the air. Now it was Hick's turn, and he took careful aim, obviously intending to kill the man who was causing so much trouble for Judge Parsons. His bullet entered the upper fleshy part of Walker's left arm, missing the bone.

Walker's conduct was extraordinary. He did not flinch, and in no way did he even indicate he had been wounded. Instead he smiled and called, "I am still alive, Mr. Hicks. Perhaps you would like to fire again."

The seconds hurriedly intervened and halted the duel.

As a result of this incident, which was widely publicized, William Walker became even more popular. He was universally regarded as one of the leaders of the reform campaign. People approached him on the streets to shake his hand, and when he appeared in a restaurant, men flocked to him. His manner was unchanged and he remained unassuming and quiet, but he must have realized, as did Edmund Randolph and others, that his status in society had changed. Californians recognized him as a leader.

But he was still restless, looking for fresh fields to conquer. The fight against crime and corruption in San Francisco promised to be a long, grinding battle, and Walker could do little but repeat himself in his editorials. After spending a little more than a year on the staff of the *Herald*, he started to look elsewhere.

His opportunity came in the form of an offer from Henry P. Watkins, a distinguished attorney with a large practice in nearby Marysville, to join him in a partnership. Walker accepted on the condition that he would engage in no research and write no briefs, but would confine himself to the one phase of the law that he enjoyed, that of appearing in court.

Still shy in private, he soon blossomed as a courtroom lawyer. A colleague, Stephen J. Field, who later became an Associate Justice of the United States Supreme Court, called the twenty-seven-year-old Walker a "brilliant speaker who could sway judges and juries alike with his rhetoric and reason."

Life in Marysville was quiet, the tedium relieved only by court appearances. The social life of the community was limited, partly because there were few married women in the town, so virtually no one entertained at home. Walker, true to his upbringing, still did not drink and refused to play cards, so there was little for him to do at night, unless he wanted to visit one of the town's many brothels.

Whether he sought the company of prostitutes is a matter of conjecture. The more romantic of his earlier biographers claim that he remained true to the memory of his beloved Ellen, but the question is debatable. At twenty-seven he was in robust health and was a popular and successful man. Experience already had altered many of his attitudes. Walking from his lodging house to his office and back each day Walker passed two of Marysville's more popular houses of prostitution, and when business lagged the girls frequently sat on the front porches of these establishments. Occasionally some of them attended court sessions to listen to Walker's fiery speeches, so a number of the girls knew him, at least by sight. It was their habit to greet passers-by, and they could not have ignored one of the most prominent men in town.

Perhaps Walker clung to his memories of Ellen and

was strong enough to reject the blandishments of the Marysville prostitutes, but it is reasonable to assume that he sometimes visited one or another of the girls.

These activities, however, would not have been sufficient to calm his restlessness. In San Francisco he had become acquainted with a French nobleman who was a kindred spirit, Count Gaston Raoul Raousset-Boulbon, and Raousset was to influence his life more than anyone he had ever met. A onetime newspaperman and novelist, a former soldier, hunter, fisherman, and miner, Raousset was as idealistic as Walker and, as events proved, as impractical.

By the latter part of 1851 Raousset had conceived of a wild venture. The lower portion of Arizona still belonged to Mexico, where it was considered a part of the state of Sonora, and the settlers there, most of them Mexicans, were plagued by frequent attacks of the formidable Apache Indians. Raousset proposed to lead an expedition to Arizona, most of his force to be made up of French citizens from San Francisco, and in return for clearing out the Apaches he hoped to win the exclusive rights to mine gold and silver in the area.

The expedition failed, in part because various Mexican officials had been bribed by San Francisco bankers, who hoped that an American expedition could win the mining rights for the United States. For that matter, it was always possible that an American expedition could annex southern Arizona and make a gift of it to the United States.

The originator of a similar scheme was William Walker, aided and abetted by his partner, Watkins. They were motivated by patriotism, and Walker, at least, had no interest in making a fortune for himself. Money, as such, had never been important to him, and was not important now.

46

Late in 1852 Raousset returned to San Francisco after his little army of 250 men had been defeated in battle attempting to capture the capital of Sonora, Hermosillo. But San Francisco greeted him as a conqueror, and one of the first to sit down in private with him was William Walker, who had, at long last, found his own true calling.

Walker proposed that they join hands in conquering Sonora.

Raousset politely declined.

Walker, privately assured of financial support by various San Francisco bankers and a number of other prominent citizens who had become his enthusiastic supporters, made it clear that regardless of whether the count intended to return to Mexico, he himself would go there.

No public announcement was made, but word spread quickly that the intrepid William Walker intended to go to Sonora, and planned, either through diplomacy or by the use of force, to wrest mining concessions from the Mexican government. A number of the city's wealthiest men, who had made their fortunes in gold, were eager to add their investments to the enterprise.

In order to find legal means to secure the funds, Walker displayed powers of inventiveness that he had never before shown. On December 1, 1852, he issued bonds in denominations of $500, in return for which the "Republic of Sonora," as he called his enterprise, would grant to the purchaser "one league of land." That land, of course, would come from the concessions he hoped to win from the Mexicans.

His imagination working overtime, Walker called himself the "Colonel of the Independent Regiment." It did not bother him or disturb his financial supporters that he was totally lacking in military experience.

Edmund Randolph became a supporter of the enterprise, and so did his law partner, Parker Crittenden. These two men were prominent in San Francisco's highest financial and social circles, and potential supporters who had hesitated no longer held back.

Walker had estimated that his expedition would cost $25,000, but in less than a week more than $50,000 had been collected, and Randolph, who had a better understanding of finance than did Walker, announced that no more bonds would be sold. A few days later Walker sailed alone for Guaymas, the principal seaport of Sonora, on board a commercial ship. He traveled alone, in civilian clothes, carrying only his sword for protection.

The military commander of the Sonora garrisons was already in Guaymas, and the governor of the province joined him there for meetings with the American. Walker, hoping to cloak his venture in a peaceful guise, told the Mexican officials that he wanted to lead a party of "colonists" to the province. He promised to rid Sonora of the dangers of Apache raids, and in return he hoped to be granted mining rights.

The Mexican authorities were not impressed by the diminutive would-be adventurer. After outlining what he had in mind Walker sat silent and ill at ease, his hands folded primly in his lap. Though only twenty-nine years old, he looked much older, and he resembled a small-town American lawyer. The truth of the matter was that he *was* a small-town American lawyer who knew literally nothing about driving away Apache Indians, establishing a colony, or exploring the mountains of Arizona for possible mines.

His visit to Guaymas did produce one positive result. A number of American families lived there, and they banded together one evening to entertain Walker at dinner. The ladies who were present told him hair-raising stories of the fate of other women and children who had been captured by the Apache bands. These unfortunates, they said, had either been murdered or forced into slavery as prostitutes.

Here was an element that had been missing from Walker's grandiose scheme. Now, when he returned to San Francisco, he would be in a position to endow his mission with something more than a commercial purpose. He would announce that he was engaging in a holy mission to protect American women and children from "the most desperate, cruel savages ever known in North America." The good ladies of Guaymas, he would announce repeatedly, had begged him to bring enough men with him to end the Apache threat for all time.

It is true that the Apache were a warlike nation, but they were not really so cruel. The reputation they achieved as the most barbaric of Indian tribes was the direct result of the propaganda that Walker disseminated. Even Kit Carson, the most renowned of Indian fighters, was taken in by it, and not until another decade and more had passed did Carson finally realize the truth and revise his opinions.

The governor, after delaying for some days, invited Walker to Hermosillo for further discussions, but the American was wary. There was nothing to be settled in Hermosillo that could not be decided in Guaymas, and he suspected that the Mexicans, once they had enticed him to visit the interior, intended to throw him into prison and allow him to languish there. He declined the invitation.

Sailing back to San Francisco, Walker knew that his

colonization plan, borrowed from the French count, would have to be abandoned. No longer could he hope to win mining grants for his investors. So he had two choices: either he would have to give up his entire scheme, or he would be compelled to lead a strictly military expedition to Sonora and conquer the province by force of arms. If he elected to take the latter course he would be violating a federal law that prohibited Americans from invading foreign territory.

William Walker did not need to ponder for very long. The lure of adventure was irresistible, and he made up his mind to lead a fighting army to Sonora. Returning to San Francisco, the would-be soldier of fortune went to work with a vengeance. He bought a sturdy ship, the *Arrow*, and with the aid of his associates began to purchase arms, food, uniforms, and other supplies.

Walker's easiest task was that of recruiting men for his army. Unemployment was a major problem in the San Francisco area, where thousands of disappointed gold seekers were unable to find work of any kind and lacked the funds for transportation back to their former homes. Among those available were veterans of the Mexican War as well as frontiersmen familiar with firearms. Walker interviewed each of his potential recruits at length and selected a company of one hundred men. Lacking military experience of any kind himself, he had the audacity and questionable judgment of making another untrained newcomer his lieutenant colonel, or second in command.

Timothy Crocker, who was only twenty years of age, had been born in Ireland and still spoke with a brogue. Tall, handsome, and slender, he had one quality that endeared him to his superior: he was a blatant hero-worshiper who believed that William Walker was the greatest of men. His appearance in history is brief. What he did prior to joining the expedition is unknown, and he vanished again after serving with Walker. It must be said for him that he was steadfast in his loyalty and, when necessary, displayed considerable courage.

By the early autumn of 1853 Walker was ready to depart. The newspapers had made no secret of his expedition, and in several interviews he exuded optimism, even though Count Raousset-Boulbon had remained in San Francisco.

The federal authorities in San Francisco took a jaundiced view of Walker's plans, and on September 30, 1853, the commanding general of the United States Army garrison was ordered to seize the *Arrow* on the grounds that its owner intended to violate federal law. All of the supplies, weapons, and ammunition for the enterprise were already on board.

Edmund Randolph went to court on Walker's behalf to obtain the release of the ship, but it was obvious that many months would pass before the issue was settled. Walker was too impatient to wait.

He purchased another vessel, the *Caroline,* purchased more supplies and guns, and secretly rounded up as many of his volunteers as he could find. Before dawn on a morning in early October of 1853, he sailed out of San Francisco Bay with an "army" of precisely forty-five men, his goal that of conquering an entire province in Mexico.

4

William Walker's contemporaries did not believe he had taken leave of whatever sense he may have possessed, but posterity cannot take his comic-opera invasion of Mexico seriously. Walker was sufficiently sane to realize that his small band could not attack the large Mexican garrison at Guaymas, so he gave up his plan to conquer Sonora, and instead concentrated on what he regarded as a more realistic goal, the subjugation of the peninsula of Lower California which was sparsely populated.

On the morning of November 3 the *Caroline* dropped anchor off the sleepy town of La Paz, the provincial capital, and the "troops" went ashore. They encountered no resistance, and the governor, an unfortunate named Espanoza, was cast into the town's jail, a mud hut with one cell.

The Mexican flag was lowered, and a new one of solid blue, with a large red star in the center, which had been designed by Walker himself, was raised over the local courthouse. Walker issued a proclamation that speaks for itself:

The Republic of Lower California is hereby declared Free, Sovereign and Independent and all allegiance to the Republic of Mexico is forever renounced.

Happily playing his game of make-believe, Walker further announced that he was president of the new republic, and he appointed a full cabinet, consisting of associates in San Francisco. The few residents of the little town of La Paz yawned and went about their usual business. Most were illiterate fishermen, and they were completely indifferent to the heroics the Yankee invader was displaying.

After a few days Walker's euphoria dissipated. His former law partner, Watkins, was supposed to be joining him with 250 reinforcements, but Mexico wasn't taking his invasion seriously.

So, after pondering the problem, he set the local governor free, took his forty-five faithful back on board the *Caroline,* and sailed to the larger town of Ensenada, about fifty miles south of the American border. There he repeated his tactics, but having no troops to spare for prison duty, he sent the governor of Lower California on board his ship for safekeeping.

This time the Mexican government responded, and two hundred troops were sent to rid the province of the nuisance. Walker had possession of the small fort overlooking the harbor, and fortunately found two small cannon there. The Mexicans attacked, he and his men fired the cannon, and the Mexicans retreated. There were no American casualties and, as far as is known, the Mexicans suffered none, either. Walker promptly issued an order of the day in which he congratulated his gallant army on its military triumph.

The following morning he looked out the window of

⌄room in the governor's palace and saw the *Caro-* putting out to sea. All of his food supplies and spare ammunition were on board. Not until later did he learn that the Mexican governor of Lower California had solved his own immediate problem and done his country a service by bribing the captain and crew of the ship, who promptly left the president of the new republic stranded.

Several days later Watkins arrived, accompanied by 230 men, aboard the *Anita.* He brought ample arms and ammunition, but carried virtually no food, so he promptly turned around and went back to San Francisco for more supplies. Walker faced his first crisis.

He was sufficiently sane to realize the inhabitants of the district would turn on him if he seized meat and grain from them. He solved his problem by attacking the camp of a Mexican outlaw and capturing his meat and corn.

The little army was growing restless. The men had nothing to occupy their time with, the diet of beef and corn was monotonous, and they resented Walker's strict order prohibiting drinking or any association with local women.

A far more serious blow to Walker's hopes developed in Mexico City, where the United States minister, James Gadsden, on December 30, 1853, concluded negotiations with the Mexican government for the purchase of that portion of Sonora province adjoining the Arizona Territory for a price of $10 million. Gadsden made it plain that his government would consider Walker an outlaw.

The Gadsden Purchase destroyed the interest of the San Francisco investors in Walker's project. The Mexican navy stationed a gunboat in the Ensenada harbor to prevent the landing of reinforcements or supplies. And the United States sent an emissary on board a warship, the *Portsmouth*, to tell Walker about the Gadsden Purchase. He was informed that his friends in San Francisco would give him no further aid, financial or otherwise, and that unless he desisted in his adventure and went home, he would be prosecuted in the federal courts whenever he returned to American soil.

William Walker was too deeply involved in his filibuster to admit defeat, and he now conceived the idea of winning the support of the natives of Lower California and Sonora, whom he would persuade to join his republic. His reasoning was simple and direct: they hated the government in Mexico City, and consequently would hail him as a liberator.

His own men balked. They were being forced to forage for food now, and were in danger of being hanged by irate ranch owners. They were deprived of the gold and silver in the Gadsden Purchase, and they had no intention of risking their lives for the glorification of William Walker. Most of them wanted to go home, and they expressed their intent in no uncertain terms.

Walker allowed them to leave, taking a fair share of the food with them, but he insisted they leave their rifles behind. His will prevailed, and more than half of his little force departed.

Walker and the 130 men who still followed him reached Sonora, and marched on foot to the Colorado River through a poverty-stricken, sparsely settled land. That he was able to make the two-hundred-mile journey is itself remarkable. Food supplies were short, shoe leather gave way, and the men were in rags. Walker refused to turn back, and the better part of his force deserted, the men returning to the United States on wn, most of them half-dead from the ordeal. ultimately the leader was forced to retrace his steps and, with a band of only thirty-four men, return to Lower California. There, at last, he was compelled to face reality. The Mexicans he had seen on his march wanted nothing to do with him and his new nation, and regarded him as just another brigand. He had no funds, and his half-starved followers were too few in number for new adventures. He had to return home.

On May 8, 1854, after a nightmare march of four days on half rations, the pathetic remnants of the Army of the Republic of Lower California and Sonora reached the border post manned by the United States Army. Ever mindful of his dignity, the commander announced that he was "Colonel" William Walker, and that he was "surrendering" his troops to the United States of America.

Walker returned to San Francisco, where a federal grand jury promptly indicted him for violation of the neutrality laws. Watkins had already been found guilty and fined $1,500, and although Walker pleaded not guilty, it was certain he would suffer the same fate. President Franklin Pierce had issued firm instructions forbidding the private invasions of countries with which the United States was at peace. Many people remained friendly with Walker, but he was astonished to discover that his stature had diminished considerably.

His trial was postponed for four months, so he tried his hand briefly at politics and attended a California Democratic convention in Sacramento, but the proceedings bored him. To earn a living, he wrote articles for the Sacramento *State Journal,* but he began to look around for something more important to do.

At this critical time a newcomer appeared in his life. Byron Cole, a wealthy and worldly New Englander, had come to San Francisco to broaden his horizons, and he began by buying one of the city's lesser newspapers, the *Commercial-Advertiser*. He offered Walker the editorship, and the hero of Lower California accepted, for reasons only he and Cole knew.

The change that had taken place in the personality of the onetime physician and attorney since the death of his beloved Ellen Martin was complete. Walker's invasion of Mexico had transformed the shy, inarticulate weakling into a giant with an insatiable appetite for adventure, as well as for the glory, excitement, and recognition that were the rewards of these experiences.

Walker had demonstrated to his own satisfaction that he had tremendous physical courage. He was impervious to the fear that paralyzed other men. Never athletic or even interested in the outdoors, he had a stamina and perseverance far greater than that of men a foot taller and a hundred pounds heavier. He was an instinctive leader who was followed, trusted, and obeyed.

He was bored by politics, as he was by journalism, because he was too restless to engage in long campaigns to influence the minds of others. Direct action produced the results he sought, and he could shrug off death, brutality, and privation in order to achieve his goals.

A romantic to the innermost fiber of his being, he undoubtedly saw himself as the equal of a Sir Walter Scott hero. It no longer mattered to him that he was breaking the law when he influenced and forced others to accept his version of right and wrong. He was skilled in logic, with an infinite capacity for rationalization, and could convince himself that he was working for the attainment of the high ideals responsible for the creation of the United States.

..y of his contemporaries shared his vision of him-
..., and it was his fortune, for better or worse, to be
living in an era when vast numbers of his fellow coun-
trymen believed in Manifest Destiny. It was the destiny
of the United States to expand, they were convinced, so
that people throughout the Western Hemisphere could
share the benefits of their civilization and their type of
government.

Walker and his followers would have been shocked
had they been told they were imperialistic brigands. It
didn't occur to him or many others that other nations
might prefer their own forms of government. The
American system was the best for the United States, so
it had to be the best for everyone. Walker felt that only
a lack of knowledge prevented the inhabitants of small,
weak nations from recognizing what they were missing,
and he regarded it as his solemn duty to enlighten the
benighted, even if he had to conquer them first.

Even those who were opposed to the methods of a
soldier of fortune in the middle of the nineteenth century did not regard such a man as a cruel despot. At the
worst he was misguided, and there was much in his
nature that people admired. Neither President Pierce's
stand against filibusters nor opposition to violence
were responsible for Walker's partial loss of popularity.
He had lost a measure of his standing for the simple
reason that his expedition to Mexico had been a failure.
People still stared at him in the streets and interrupted
his meals in restaurants to shake his hand, and gradually, after a short sojourn in San Francisco and Marysville,
it occurred to him that he still retained a substantial
residue of popular goodwill.

So the time was ripe for another adventure, and Cole,
who had spent several months in Nicaragua traveling

from the East to California, convinced him that American intervention was a necessity there.

An unceasing civil war was being waged in Nicaragua in an effort to unseat President Fruto Chamorro, who was supported by the wealthy plantation owners and the British. Chamorro, who had made himself dictator, was opposed to a federation of Nicaragua with her neighbors, El Salvador and Honduras. The revolutionaries, who were known as Liberals, were supported by Honduras. But that country could do little to oust Chamorro and his Conservatives because his friends in Guatemala and Costa Rica, also dictatorships where British influence was strong, would have attacked Honduras at the first sign of interference. It occurred to few people that Great Britain and, to a lesser extent, the United States were making it impossible for the nations of Central America to work out their own destinies in their own way.

Cole called Nicaragua a land of milk and honey and painted an alluring picture of it for Walker. The soil was rich, and almost any crop could be grown there in abundance. Cattle thrived there. Gold and silver waited to be taken from the mountains, not to mention enormous deposits of copper, zinc, and other metals. The tropical forests of the interior were overflowing with mahogany and cedar, and there was an unlimited market in the United States for both woods.

William Walker needed little persuasion. The natural resources of Nicaragua should be used to alleviate the extreme poverty of the people. The establishment of an American protectorate and an American brand of government would end the incessant revolutions that took so many lives and caused so much suffering. It was his solemn, sacred duty to lead an army of volunteers to

..gua, and after he achieved victory, popular sup-
.. in the United States for his venture would force the
Administration in Washington to recognize and help
people who had emerged from the grip of tyrants.

What Walker and Cole either ignored or did not know
was that at least one American was well aware of Nicaragua's potential. Commodore Vanderbilt, with the tacit
approval of Washington and the quiet support of London, was busily building his own empire there. He had
taken title to millions of acres of land, and his plans for
cutting a canal across the lower portion of the country
were well advanced. Because President Chamorro
represented stability, the pragmatic Vanderbilt quietly
supported him.

Cole had his private reasons for suggesting Walker's
intervention in Nicaragua. The young financier was one
of the owners of a company that had been formed to
exploit the mineral wealth of Honduras, and the government of that small country was in danger of falling.
If Chamorro extended his grip on his own country and
ended the rebellion, his friends would come to power
in Honduras, too. That meant the British would move
in, and Cole's company would be expelled. It was important to him that the rebels succeed in Nicaragua so
his own next-door interests could be preserved.

Time had not dimmed Walker's hatred of Great Bri-
tian, and to him the British, still flouting the Monroe
Doctrine, were the real villains in Central America. If he
could cause the downfall of the Chamorro regime, he
reasoned, he would be striking a mortal blow at British
influence in the area. The President and the Congress
of the United States vacillated, but Walker would do for
his country what its government appeared unwilling to
do for itself.

60

As the new editor of the *Commercial-Advertiser,* Walker took charge of the newspaper, and his crisp policy quickly increased the circulation. Cole, knowing he had left his property in competent hands, sailed to Nicaragua to glean what additional information he could about the political situation there.

During Cole's absence, in the autumn of 1854, Walker came to trial before the federal court in San Francisco. Edmund Randolph represented him, but for all practical purposes he acted as his own attorney. Never had he been more eloquent. A corrupt regime in Mexico City, he declared, was depriving the people of Lower California and Sonora of their God-given liberty and inherent right to earn a living. American ladies in Guaymas had begged him for his protection. He had failed only because the unwarranted intervention of the United States government had prevented him from receiving the supplies and reinforcements he had needed.

Above all, he based his appeal on the American precedent: "Our Pilgrim Fathers came to a savage land, rescued it from savages and made it an abode of civilization." Therefore, he regarded it as his duty to do what the Pilgrims had done, and anyone who opposed his noble cause rejected the traditions on which the United States had been built.

The expressions on the faces of the jury indicated that they agreed with the valiant Walker, and the federal prosecutor argued against him in vain. Retiring for a brief eight and a half minutes at the end of the trial, the jury returned with the verdict: Not guilty. William Walker was exonerated, and each member of the jury shook his hand, as did the judge.

At that moment Walker's rehabilitation was complete. Men who had avoided him were eager to be seen in his company again, and crowds followed him everywhere. Even rival newspaper editors felt compelled to write that he was the most popular man in San Francisco.

Rumors began to circulate to the effect that Walker would lead another expedition to stamp out tyranny. No one knew his destination or why he had chosen it, but the adventurous required no details. Within two weeks of the trial's conclusion more than five hundred men had applied to Walker for permission to join him. He smiled and said nothing, refusing to admit that he was even contemplating becoming a filibuster again, but he kept a careful list of the volunteers' names and addresses.

At the beginning of November, Cole returned from Nicaragua, carrying a letter signed by the chief of the rebels, Francisco de Castellon, who promised him a large grant of land if he would supply three hundred armed men who would fight for the cause of the Liberals against President Chamorro.

Lawyer Walker had learned a lesson in legality, and said this document was insufficient to protect the expedition from the harassment of the United States government. What was needed, he said, was a formal grant from the present government of Nicaragua, giving to one or more American sponsors the title to a tract of land and authorizing its colonization. Even then, he declared, great care would need to be exercised. If Washington learned that a military expedition was being planned under the guise of a colonizing venture, ships and provisions would be seized and the leaders of the scheme would face certain prosecution.

Cole had no choice but to return to Nicaragua. Prior to his departure he sold the *Commercial-Advertiser*, having lost interest in the newspaper. Walker promptly resigned, but took a position as editor of the Sacramento *State Democratic Journal,* which was delighted to obtain his services. He was universally regarded as an exceptionally able newspaperman, and many people predicted he would be elected to Congress or even become governor.

Certainly Walker could have achieved power through legitimate political means, but he threw away the chance with the same nonchalance with which he had given up his careers in medicine and the law. Romantic adventure was in his blood, and a seat in the United States House of Representatives would have been too tame for him.

Early in 1855 Cole returned from his second trip to Nicaragua, bringing with him a formal contract signed by Castellon. The rebel leader had no real authority, to be sure, but the tract of land he assigned to Cole was located in an area his troops controlled, so it might be regarded as a legitimate deal. Everything depended on the interpretation of the federal authorities in San Francisco, to whom it had to be submitted before an expedition would be permitted to sail.

The army officers stationed at the Presidio, San Francisco's fort, were not fools, and neither were the representatives of the Justice Department. Certainly they would realize that a document signed by a rebel leader authorizing William Walker to bring three hundred "colonists" to Nicaragua had a hidden meaning, and that meaning was not difficult to find. Walker's past spoke for itself.

The timing of Walker's new expedition inadvertently came to his rescue. Spain's grip on her few remaining possessions in the New World was loosening, and many

Americans, particularly in the South, saw a new opportunity to annex Cuba. They were opposed by Northerners who were more afraid than ever that Cuba might become a slaveholding state.

But there was a loophole, and Secretary of War Jefferson Davis, who six years later, after the outbreak of the Civil War, was to become President of the Confederacy, was quick to grasp it. A relaxation in the application of the neutrality laws might give the United States an opening in the Caribbean. Ultimately this same approach could be applied to Cuba, and the annexation could be accomplished in spite of the opposition of the Abolitionists.

The commanders of the Presidio chose to regard William Walker's colonization plan as innocent, and both the general in charge and his chief of staff, according to legend, wished Walker well. The government of San Francisco was filled with the filibuster's admirers, and they carefully looked the other way. Only the Justice Department stood between Walker and his venture, and officials there did not choose to fight him alone. They pretended the colonizing plan was genuine, and did not question the legality of a contract signed by a rebel leader who represented no government and had no real right to offer grants of Nicaraguan land to anyone.

The road to destiny was clear.

Walker no longer had any need to act in secret, so he conducted his recruiting campaign in the open after resigning from his position in Sacramento. Every newspaper printed stories about his coming expedition, and so many hundreds of men applied for places that Cole had to hire an office in which to screen them.

Walker insisted on interviewing each candidate himself, and for once in his life he demonstrated remarkable patience. His Mexican adventure had given him new insights into human nature, and he chose his subordinates with care, rejecting the boastful, the drinkers, and those who might be attracted by women. He hired a pretty girl to work in the office with him, and any would-be recruit who ogled her or tried to flirt with her was turned away.

The venture was plagued at the outset by a lack of funds. Cole was short of cash, and Walker himself was virtually penniless, as usual. But he did the best he could with limited resources. He bought an old ship, the *Vesta*, which Edmund Randolph told him was unseaworthy, and purchased only limited quantities of arms, food, and medical supplies.

What encouraged him was the caliber of some of his lieutenants. Colonel C. C. Hornsby, a hero of the Mexican War who also knew Nicaragua well, elected to join him, as did another seasoned Mexican War veteran, Major Frank Anderson. The party even boasted a physician of stature, Dr. Alexander Jones. Not the least important of the group was a soldier of fortune, hard-bitten Achilles Kewan, who had taken part in all three of Narciso López's attempts to invade Cuba. The hero-worshiping Timothy Crocker signed on again as Walker's personal aide. These men were the heart of the officers' corps, and would have done credit to any army.

William Walker's problem was that his army was pitifully small. His attempts to obtain large sums from potential investors failed, largely because the wealthy thought chances of obtaining a substantial return for their money were slim. Everyone cheered Walker, but the cash flow was only a thin trickle. Consequently, although he could have led one thousand men had the money been available, he was able to muster only a comic-opera force of precisely fifty-six men.

A less romantic leader would have abandoned his project and gone into politics. The undaunted Walker refused to be discouraged, however. Soon the entire United States would join in calling him and his companions "the immortals."

5

The departure of the immortals on their voyage to eternal glory was delayed, ingloriously, because William Walker went into debt shortly before he was scheduled to sail, and his creditors attached his only assets, the *Vesta* and her contents. Walker promptly went ashore, where he persuaded his creditors to forgive his debts. Then the sheriff demanded $300 as a fee.

The outraged Walker had no intention of paying it, and on the night of May 3, 1855, he offered the deputy sheriff left on board as a guard the choice of champagne or handcuffs. The man sensibly chose the former, and went ashore on board the pilot boat.

The lack of discipline on board ship deeply disturbed real military men like Hornsby and Anderson. The troops were insolent; they flagrantly disobeyed orders and seemed to regard themselves as partners in a lark. Walker, who had acquired a reputation as a martinet in Mexico, revealed his own lack of experience during the month-long voyage to Nicaragua. His only concerns, his principal subordinates discovered, were abstinence and assurance that ladies would not be molested. Before landing he read an order to his "army," saying that any soldier who drank would be discharged and any who annoyed a woman would be shot.

On June 1 the *Vesta* cast anchor in the harbor Realejo, a tiny port in northern Nicaragua a short distance from the city of León, the rebel capital. Walker paraded his troops through the village, and the inhabitants cheered because the newcomers were going to aid the cause of the Liberals. That night the Americans ignored the instructions of "Colonel" Walker, and the taverns did a lively business, as did the brothels. The invasion of Nicaragua was under way.

Walker himself fell in love with Nicaragua, and to the end of his short life it fascinated him. As he himself wrote, the flowers, the trees, the very air he breathed convinced him he had entered Paradise.

The following day he traveled to León for a meeting with Castellon. The rebel leader was nervously anticipating a battle with the best of the enemy commanders, General Ponciano Corral, who was marching north with his army. The Americans had come just in time.

But Walker had no intention of allowing his troops to languish in León, a charming, Spanish-flavored city with a population of about 25,000. There were too many taverns there, too many brothels, too many pretty girls wandering through the streets. Soldiers who had nothing better to do, he said, would fall into temptation.

He had an idea that demonstrated imagination. He wanted to move his little force south to the area known as the Transit, where traveling Americans journeyed overland between the Atlantic and the Pacific. Vast numbers of fortune seekers were still going from the Eastern seaboard to California and Oregon, and Walker hoped to persuade the physically fit who were adventure-minded to join his corps. He had learned in Mexico that a force of fifty-six men was too small to be effective, and he was eager to augment it.

Castellon, who Walker privately thought was too weak and indecisive to lead a revolution, agreed to lend him two hundred Nicaraguan troops. But trouble developed when the commander of the revolutionary army, General Muñoz, who wore a gorgeous uniform of gold, scarlet, and blue, insisted that the Americans place themselves under his command in León to await the arrival of the enemy.

William Walker was incapable of placing himself under the command of any man, competent or otherwise, and he had already decided that Muñoz was a clown. Rather than serve under anyone, he said, he would return to the United States and take his men with him.

Castellon gave in, and Walker made an enemy of Muñoz.

Instead of the two hundred Nicaraguan reinforcements he had been promised, he received only one hundred, and the supplies he needed, particularly flour, vegetables, and fruit, were not forthcoming. Nevertheless, he was determined to take the town of Rivas, an inland community that was a key to the western end of the Transit. He and his force of 156 men sailed south on the *Vesta,* then marched inland. A tropical rainstorm halted the little corps, so the approach to Rivas had to be made the following morning in broad daylight.

Approximately five hundred defenders lined the walls of Rivas, and it immediately became apparent that General Muñoz had notified the enemy of Walker's plans. The Nicaraguan troops who had joined the expedition promptly deserted and fled into the jungle, which left fifty-six men to do battle with five hundred.

69

The Americans opened fire as they advanced. Most of the men were sharpshooters, and they displayed almost uncanny skill as they decimated the ranks of the defenders. The Nicaraguans were poor shots, but made up in numbers what they lacked in accuracy. Six of Walker's men were killed, among them Crocker and Kewen.

The attackers fought their way to a large house, where they barricaded themselves inside. Five of the Americans were wounded and had to be left outside. Their comrades were enraged when they saw the Nicaraguans bayoneting these helpless men.

In the hours that followed, the Americans suffered no more casualties, but picked off almost two hundred of the enemy, and it appeared that in spite of the odds against them they might be victorious. But the Conservatives obtained a small cannon and bombarded the house, making its evacuation necessary. Walker waited until evening, then he and his men made a run for it. They escaped and marched back through the jungle to the *Vesta*, which transported them safely to Realejo.

The defeat, caused in the main by treachery and by the reduction of Walker's force to forty-five men, a number of whom were wounded, would have discouraged most soldiers. It had the opposite effect on Walker and his men. They had survived the ordeal, and they were determined to obtain vengeance, no matter what the cost.

Dr. Jones attended the wounded, aided by Walker, who wrote a firm letter to Castellon, telling him in blunt language what had happened and demanding the immediate discharge of General Muñoz. Castellon responded by begging Walker to come to the defense of León as soon as his men were fit.

The little corps was heartened when Byron Cole arrived in Realejo from Honduras with twenty volunteers. Nineteen were American and the twentieth proved to be the most valuable member of the entire expedition. Captain Bruno von Netzmer, a clean-shaven man like Walker, who had several dueling scars on his face, was a former Prussian cavalry officer. He had spent six years in Nicaragua as a soldier, businessman, and investor, and he was thoroughly familiar with the country.

His advice was priceless. It was essential, he said, for Walker to obtain the support of the Roman Catholic hierarchy.

Walker did as von Netzmer suggested. He went out of his way to establish friendships with the clergy, a task he found easy because he soon discovered that he and they held virtually identical opinions about the morality of the people and the need to bolster it.

Captain von Netzmer was also responsible for instructing Walker in the psychology of the people, who had grown weary of civil war in the thirty-four years of Nicaragua's independence. They believed that all politicians were corrupt and that all political parties sought power for themselves, regardless of their labels. Above all, von Netzmer said, the only Nicaraguan soldier worthy of being called a fighting man was the volunteer. Both armies were filled with conscripts who were useless in battle, and who would flee from the field at the first sound of gunfire. When convinced of the worthiness of a cause, however, the Nicaraguan troops were courageous, loyal, and completely trustworthy.

Walker led his little band to León, fearing treachery, and he soon discovered he was right. His corps was surrounded by the troops of the treacherous General Muñoz, and the American felt compelled to issue an ultimatum to Castellon. Either the Nicaraguans were

71

removed, or he would regard them as an enemy force and would act accordingly.

The Nicaraguans disappeared, and Walker, acting on the advice of his Prussian aide, moved his corps to the nearby town of Chinandega, whose people were growing tired of Castellon's vacillations. There he won the support of two prominent members of the community, Thomas Manning, a plantation owner and retired British diplomat, and a middle-aged Italian named José Vallé.

Manning became Walker's firm admirer, but Vallé was even more important to him. Vallé, who weighed three hundred pounds, was a former colonel in the Liberal army and the most influential man in the area. He and Walker took to each other at first sight and soon established a genuine friendship, the first Walker had known since his association with Edmund Randolph.

Within a short time Vallé began to recruit Nicaraguans for the American corps. Thanks to his persuasiveness they believed in the purity of Walker's motives, and soon proved themselves dependable. When 125 of them had enlisted, word of the development reached León, and Castellon grew alarmed, particularly because General Muñoz, his closest associate, had died of a heart attack, and he himself now felt vulnerable and exposed.

Castellon ordered Walker to disband his native company and return without delay to León. Instead, completely ignoring the command, Walker went with all of his men to Realejo, where they boarded the *Vesta* and sailed to the little port of San Juan del Sur.

There Walker learned that a large enemy force was gathering in the interior to destroy him. He and his corps, numbering about 65 Americans and the 125

Nicaraguans under the command of Vallé, marched inland to Virgin Bay, the principal harbor, which was owned and operated by the Accessory Transit Company on Lake Nicaragua. Walker occupied the highest ground, which included the warehouses and offices of the Transit Company, and prepared to meet the foe.

He did not have long to wait. Early the next morning an army of 600 Conservatives launched an attack on his positions. Both sides had no weapons other than rifles, and the entrenched Americans and their Nicaraguan comrades not only held superior positions but were far better marksmen. After fire had been exchanged for about three hours the Conservatives fled, leaving about sixty dead and more than one hundred wounded on the field.

Walker's casualties were astonishingly light: two of his Nicaraguans had been killed, and one of his Americans had suffered a slight wound. His men began to regard themselves as invincible. Equally significant, Walker had exposed himself repeatedly to enemy fire, which no Nicaraguan commander had ever done, and a spent bullet had grazed the side of his neck, leaving no mark. His Nicaraguans were convinced he had a charmed life.

The importance of Walker's victory at Virgin Bay cannot be overestimated. His little army had defeated a force three times its size, and the entire country was impressed.

That same day word came from León that Chamorro, the Conservative dictator, had died suddenly of cholera, and that Castellon had fallen victim to the same disease. Nicaragua was in chaos.

The following day, while Walker pondered his next move, a party of forty American recruits joined his

73

band. His entire force now numbered about 230, so he decided to take the offensive. After sundown he loaded his entire corps onto a lake steamer and sailed for Granada, the national capital and Conservative stronghold.

Walker landed near the gracious old city and attacked the garrison before dawn. A flag of surrender was raised after only a few shots had been fired. There were no casualties on either side, and Walker later wrote that "the encounter could scarcely be dignified with the name of action."

By sunrise his forces had occupied the government buildings, and he controlled not only Granada but the fertile farm and plantation valley that stretched all the way to Léon. With almost absurd ease William Walker had ended the revolution and made himself the undisputed master of Nicaragua.

His first order to his victorious troops forbade looting, rape, and intoxication. For the first time he signed himself as "General" William Walker, and he meant his command to be taken literally. An American soldier who made the mistake of molesting an Indian girl was tried by a court-martial within the hour, led before a firing squad, and executed.

Walker and his immediate subordinates took up residence in the presidential palace, and his entire situation was changed. He held a meeting with John N. Wheeler, the United States Minister to Nicaragua, who offered him unqualified support. The British minister was friendly, the Accessory Transit Company backed him, and the wealthy citizens of Granada flocked to his side.

That Sunday, November 21, 1855, he attended mass at the cathedral, and later held a long discussion with the pastor, Father Augustin Vijil, who became his friend. A few days later the vicar-general of the See of Nicaragua wrote Walker an official letter of congratulation and made him a "loan" of a thousand ounces of silver.

Newspapers in the United States filled their front pages with the story of Walker's triumph. As a direct result of this and later publicity, more than fifteen hundred American volunteers joined his forces within the next year.

Granada, with a population of only fifteen thousand, was smaller than León, but far more sophisticated, boasting excellent shops and restaurants, concert halls and hotels. The poor were as poverty-stricken as they were elsewhere in the country, but the wealthy lived in comfort as great as that enjoyed by the aristocrats of Europe.

A member of one of the leading families became Walker's mentor and counselor, and she was the first woman who had been close to him since Ellen Martin. Doña Irena Ohoran, whose Irish grandfather had spelled the name "O'Horan," was tiny, vivacious, and exceptionally attractive. In her midtwenties and unmarried, she took Walker everywhere, and acted as his sponsor when presenting the country's financial land agricultural leaders to him.

It was inevitable that rumors should arise concerning a romance between the dashing Walker and the lovely Irena, but they were probably untrue. His puritanical nature would not have permitted such indulgence with a woman. Furthermore, although few people knew it, Irena was already deeply involved in a romance with Narciso Espinoza, a wealthy Nicaraguan prominent in the Conservative party.

However, Walker may have developed something of

a personal interest in Irena. For all practical purposes, he was the ruler of Nicaragua from the time he captured Granada, and he worked from six o'clock in the morning until at least ten o'clock at night, sometimes remaining at his desk in the palace or in conferences until midnight and later. His only relief was a daily horseback ride for an hour or two, and he invariably was accompanied on these canters by Irena.

The American press, magnifying every detail of Walker's life, tried to make more of his relationship than the facts warranted. Some irresponsible newspapers, which spelled Irena's name in a variety of ways, flatly suggested that she was Walker's mistress, but no concrete evidence of it exists today. Furthermore, Walker continued to insist that his American officers and troops refrain from consorting with Nicaraguan women, and many of his men resented this decree. A number of them ultimately deserted him and returned home because they found it too difficult to obey such an order. Since nothing in Walker's day-to-day existence could have been kept secret, particularly from the officers who were living under the same roof with him, they undoubtedly would have known it had he been engaging in an affair with Irena.

Obviously it would have been impossible for Walker to demand that the others live according to one standard while he observed another. Even the most loyal of his subordinates would have rebelled. They were volunteers who subjected themselves to his authority willingly, and had his conduct been hypocritical they would have abandoned him.

Walker's stand against consorting with local women caused so many problems that he was eventually compelled to relax the rule somewhat and permit his troops

76

to visit brothels, provided they paid the inmates for their services. Class differences were so marked in Nicaragua that there were separate houses of prostitution for the rich and the poor. The officers went to the former, the enlisted men to the latter, and diaries kept by some of the senior officers of the command indicated that, on infrequent occasions, Walker himself went with them.

Irena's motives for associating with Walker could have been very simple. In the absence of any letters that may have shown she was personally drawn to him, we can only conclude she had a far more crass reason for going for a daily ride with him. She was a wealthy property owner; he was the most powerful man in her country. By making him her friend, she was protecting her estates and their crops of sugar, bananas, and vegetables.

Years later, after Walker's departure from Nicaragua, Irena Ohoran married Espinoza. This fact alone should be enough to silence the gossips and the early biographers.

Walker's first policy decision after capturing Granada was of paramount importance. The Liberals confidently expected him to order a bloodbath of their defeated opponents, but Walker had developed a political acumen previously conspicuous by its absence from his character. The man who had written inflammatory antislavery editorials in New Orleans, who had defied public opinion and the law in San Francisco, became the great conciliator. It was time, he reasoned, for the Nicaraguans to end their civil war and for the political factions to make their peace with each other and work together for the development of a country whose potential had yet to be realized. Consequently he refused to prosecute his former enemies and sent no Conservatives to the firing squad or sentenced them to prison.

Firmly holding his Liberal supporters in check, Walker insisted on the formation of a national government that would include members of both parties. He rejected all plans to expropriate the property of the principal supporters of the Conservatives, and at the same time he insisted that the Liberals be given recognition for their patriotic efforts.

The Conservatives were ecstatic and immediately became his unwavering supporters. The more bloodthirsty of the Liberals were disappointed, but his power and prestige were so great they did not dare oppose him.

Wheeler, the American minister, openly applauded. So did Thomas Manning, Walker's friend, who had just been appointed Great Britain's acting minister. Business interests were behind him, including the Anglo-American-owned Accessory Transit Company. The press in the United States, relieved because it could concentrate on something other than the mounting crisis over slavery, hailed Walker as a hero of heroes.

Only Commodore Vanderbilt kept his own counsel and awaited further developments before deciding where he stood.

If Walker had wished, he could have proclaimed himself President of Nicaragua, and it would have been an easy task for him to assume supreme powers as a dictator. Acting with great caution, however, and adopting a modest pose that may or may not have been genuine, he announced that he would accept neither the presidency nor a cabinet position. These places, he declared, should be taken by Nicaraguans.

For the present, and strictly in order to ensure that

the peace would be kept, Walker said, he would take the position of commander in chief of the army, and he would hold it no longer than he deemed necessary. He would attend cabinet meetings, to be sure, but only in an "advisory" capacity.

His unassuming stance did not fool any Nicaraguan who was politically sophisticated. No matter what titles Walker took, no matter what position he rejected, he was the country's only real power. Officeholders, no matter what their rank, would be required to defer to his wishes.

As usual, however, Walker meant precisely what he said. While the political situation was being sorted out, a process that occupied the better part of his time, he consolidated the Liberal and Conservative armies, for the present allowing each unit to retain its own officers. Meanwhile, his own American corps continued to grow, and he carefully kept it under his own command. His sharpshooters, foreigners all, retained the ultimate balance of power.

His unassailable high morality won him the unstinting support of the Church, and Nicaragua's three bishops became his unofficial counselors. Even they were sometimes surprised by the fervor of his puritanism, and they were successful in their efforts to persuade him not to take too firm a stand. Thanks to their influence, the taverns were not closed, and Walker was dissuaded from issuing a decree banning the national pastime, cockfighting, which he loathed.

In private Walker soon concluded that each of the Central American republics was too small and weak to assert itself and direct its own affairs. These countries should unite, he believed. They should first form a confederation, gradually give their powers to a central government, and ultimately band together as one nation under one flag, preferably his flag.

But he knew better than to express such opinions to anyone except Byron Cole, his political deputy, and Colonel Hornsby, his military deputy. Great Britain, with widespread economic holdings in the area, would become alarmed at the idea and try to unseat him. The United States, with its growing interests, would be equally unhappy. And he knew he would make enemies of the politicians in Costa Rica, Guatemala, and Honduras. As nearly as can be ascertained, Commodore Vanderbilt did not enter into Walker's calculations.

General Walker's first step was that of making peace with the Conservative commander, General Ponciano Corral. Demonstrating hitherto unsuspected shrewdness, he allowed Corral to prepare the written agreement, then quietly added amendments and made changes that would achieve the result he wanted, that of forming a single national army. To the surprise of many, the pompous Corral became his friend and supporter.

Walker solved the dilemma of the presidency by rounding up the political leaders of both parties, sitting them down together in a palace chamber and then deliberately absenting himself while they discussed the problem. It was clear that he would accept no violent partisan of either faction, so they finally compromised and settled on Don Patricio Rivas, an elderly Conservative who had joined no party and had minded his own business through the years.

Rivas took the oath of office as President on December 1, 1855, with Walker standing beside him on the steps of the cathedral. Cannon boomed, bands played, and the consolidated military forces passed in review.

General Corral was made Minister of War. He assumed he would be in charge of the armed forces, but he soon discovered that he was badly mistaken. Walker kept the army under his own firm control, and the Minister of War was only a figurehead.

The disappointed Corral wrote a secret letter to the new dictator of Honduras and urged that Honduras, Guatemala, and El Salvador immediately intervene in Nicaragua's affairs. He suggested that he would welcome it if they mounted a joint invasion.

The messenger to whom Corral gave the letter happened to be one of Walker's veterans, so the damning evidence ended up in Walker's hands. Walker wasted no time. He presented the document to Corral at a cabinet meeting, and the Minister of War was forced to admit he had written it.

By neither temperament nor intellectual background was the puritanical William Walker able to accept the Central American penchant for conspiracy and counterconspiracy. A more sophisticated manipulator might have pretended to be unaware of what was happening, and then have neutralized Corral through assassination. Walker, however, openly accused him of treason and demanded that President Rivas take action accordingly.

The cabinet decided that Corral should be judged by a court-martial, the board to be composed only of American officers. Of course, the court could render only one verdict—guilty—and it ordered that the Minister of War be executed.

The officers concluded the trial with an appeal to Walker, urging that he show clemency, and Walker consulted his conscience. He could reach only one conclusion: Corral was a traitor and could be shown no mercy.

Therefore, on December 8, 1855, the Minister of War was executed in a Granada plaza by a firing squad.

This incident caused the first upsurge of anti-Walker feeling in Nicaragua. Corral had been popular in Conservative circles, where many had expected Walker to behave like a butcher. He had acted accordingly, and although he had solidified his own position, he had made his first real enemies in Nicaragua. Even Irena Ohoran became more reserved in her attitude toward him, and she no longer accompanied him on his daily canter.

Although he had sown seeds of hatred in Nicaragua, Walker was applauded in the United States, Great Britain, and France. He was emerging as the first genuine strong figure Central American politics had seen in years, and editorials in all three countries variously referred to him as a "great man," "a great leader," and "an incorruptible hero."

Far more significant was the reaction of the other small Central American republics. Without exception they were ruled by right-wing strongmen, all of whom looked apprehensively in Walker's direction. He wanted their friendship, if only to buy time for himself to put Nicaragua's affairs in order, and he wrote cordial letters to all of them. Only El Salvador, the weakest and most timid of Nicaragua's neighbors, deigned to reply. Honduras, Costa Rica, and Guatemala remained silent.

General Maximo Jerez, one of the more prominent Liberal commanders, proposed to Walker that he might gain the support of liberals throughout Central America if he went on the offensive and toppled the regimes of the dictators. General Trinidad Cabañas, the leader of the Liberals in Honduras, who were now out of power, came to Granada to second Jerez's proposal.

Walker listened to the pair, but decided against taking their advice. His own instinct told him that public opinion in the other Central American republics would turn against him if he acted as the aggressor. It would be far better, he said, to let the others attack him first. Then, as the defender of the right and the good, he would be able to rally the support of all factions in every country.

Walker's Anglo-Saxon reasoning was contrary to the way men acted in Central America. Leaders of every party sought power for its own sake, regardless of the political label they used, and when out of power they took violent action to gain it. Therefore, Walker's attitude was incomprehensible to Jerez and Cabañas, who retired to León in a sulk. The only conclusion they could draw was that his real reason for rejecting their request was a desire to consolidate his own personal position in Nicaragua. It did not occur to them that he might be sincere.

So Walker had made new, powerful enemies, and the list would grow. The former physician, lawyer, and newspaperman, who had had no experience and no training for his present post, was discovering the difficulties of maintaining one's balance on a windswept mountain peak.

6

Some of William Walker's fondest dreams had come true in Nicaragua, suddenly and literally overnight, but he craved more than the applause of an illiterate, poverty-stricken Latin American people. Above all, he wanted recognition in the United States for his exploits.

One of his men, a Californian who had worked for him in San Francisco as a printer, came to him in Granada one day with an astonishing revelation. The man had learned that a printing press, complete with newsprint and ink, was gathering dust in a warehouse on Lake Nicaragua. Walker made inquiries and discovered that the story was true. The equipment had been in transit from the Eastern seaboard of the United States to California, but had been abandoned because the people who had ordered it had gone bankrupt.

Walker ordered the equipment brought to Granada and housed in a building he had erected for the purpose. A sign over the door indicated that this was the home of *El Nicaraguense*, a new daily newspaper. The publisher was none other than Byron Cole, and the production director was his former printer, who trained several local people to assist him. A number of young Nicaraguans and two members of the American community in Granada were hired as writers. Neither then nor later was the name of the editor ever made public.

The newspaper was unique because it was bilingual, each item printed in both Spanish and English in parallel columns. From the time of its first appearance in mid-December, 1855, *El Nicaraguense* was recognized in Nicaragua as William Walker's mouthpiece, and every literate citizen read it daily and with care. Walker saw to it that copies of every edition were sent by ship to the major newspapers in New York, Boston, Philadelphia, Baltimore, and San Francisco, and as a result, his publicity in the United States quadrupled. All of his doings were covered, and they were almost always presented in a favorable light.

At first Walker wrote editorials for his new newspaper anonymously, even though his identity as the author was an open secret. Eventually, learning that *El Nicaraguense* was a valuable instrument in notifying the United States government and powerful financial interests back home of his stand on various issues, Walker let the newspaper assume a far more official attitude. When he said something he deemed really important, he signed the article with his name.

From the outset the circulation was large, and the enterprise was by far the most successful of Walker's newspapers. He thought advertising might impair the dignity of *El Nicaraguense,* so it carried none. But it was widely read in Granada, León, and the smaller cities of Nicaragua, as well as in the United States. At times, when Walker was making active news, many American newspapers devoted their entire front pages to his activities, which were many and varied, colorful and dramatic.

Walker had funds of his own to pay his American troops, but the Nicaraguan national treasury was empty, having been looted by various generals and politicians. The Accessory Transit Company came to his rescue and lent him $20,000 in cash. They promised to send him an additional five hundred men from the United States, in return for his pledge that the travel route between the oceans would remain open and that passengers would be safe.

The intermediary in this deal was an old acquaintance of Walker from Sacramento, Parker French. French, who wore a full beard, was a onetime newspaper publisher. He was also a soldier of fortune, and he had lost an arm fighting in Mexico. Walker had no way of knowing he was a scoundrel.

French pressed for his reward in the Transit Company deal, demanding to be made Nicaragua's Minister to the United States. Walker preferred to give that post to a distinguished Nicaraguan, and he made his first mistake when he had French appointed Minister of Lands and Homes. The new cabinet member plunged into his duties with zeal, expropriating choice property all over Nicaragua and putting it under his own name. As Walker himself later wrote in his book, *The War in Nicaragua*, "French's rapacity made him dreaded by the people."

The land French stole was returned to its rightful owners, but feelings against him ran so high that he was in danger of being lynched. Walker, his sponsor, had to send him out of the country without delay, and somehow save face for himself. Therefore, much against his own better judgment, Walker sent the wily rascal to

Washington as Nicaragua's minister.

Meanwhile, another related problem arose when a Texan, Colonel Henry Kinney, landed on the Mosquito Coast with a party of "colonists," took possession of Greytown (San Juan del Norte) and claimed a large piece of Nicaraguan territory as his own. He tried to make a deal whereby he and Walker would join forces, and Walker responded by threatening to hang him.

Other Americans arranged a temporary truce, and the two men met. Walker was still seething, and he refused to have anything to do with a person who was trying to make a fortune at the expense of the Nicaraguan people, so Kinney went to President Rivas. Kinney made an attempt to persuade Rivas to drop Walker, claiming he was a greedy conniver. Rivas replied that he had placed the defense of his country in the hands of General Walker.

Kinney was expelled from the country, and his followers promptly joined Walker's legion. Kinney went to Washington, where he complained to the State Department and influential members of Congress that Walker was violating the neutrality laws.

Meanwhile, the wily French was recruiting for Walker with more enthusiasm than skill, and hundreds of volunteers were sailing for Nicaragua from New York and San Francisco. The Administration in Washington was embarrassed and tried to enforce the neutrality laws more firmly. Walker was even more embarrassed, although he was beyond the reach of the United States government. He dismissed French and appointed Father Vijil as minister in his place. French went to New Orleans, then traveled through the South collecting money from contributors who thought they were supporting Walker. Finally it became necessary for *El*

Nicaraguense to print a notice stating that French had no connection with the government of Nicaragua or with General Walker.

William Walker was learning that more than raw courage was needed if a man in a place of great power wanted to maintain his balance. Certainly he needed more than courage to deal with a major crisis that erupted at the end of 1855.

Commodore Vanderbilt, acting with vigor and stealth, had gained financial control of the Accessory Transit Company from Cornelius K. Garrison, the former mayor of San Francisco, who was Walker's old friend. Garrison countered with a clever scheme of his own. Enlisting the aid of Edmund Randolph, he sent Walker's oldest and best friend to Nicaragua to urge him to seize the company's assets because it was heavily in debt to the government of Nicaragua. Then, according to the plan, Randolph would persuade Walker to turn the company over to Garrison, who "could be trusted."

Walker was delighted to see Randolph, and he gave a dinner in his honor which was attended by President Rivas and the entire cabinet. The following day the old friends got down to business, with Randolph arguing that the Accessory Transit Company's charter had been nullified because it had failed to live up to its financial obligations to the government of Nicaragua.

While these discussions were in progress, Commodore Vanderbilt, who knew nothing about them, was engaged in buying additional Transit Company stock in New York.

Walker agreed with Randolph's argument. He canceled the Transit Company's charter, seized its property, and turned all of it over to Garrison under a new charter. This strange act has mystified historians for a century and a quarter.

Walker's right to take such action cannot be questioned. It was his prerogative, as a high-ranking official of the Nicaraguan government, to do what he thought best for the welfare of that country. On a practical basis, however, he must have realized he was juggling sticks of burning dynamite. Commodore Vanderbilt was one of the wealthiest, most powerful financiers in the United States, and Walker was sufficiently intelligent to realize he would make a mortal enemy of a man whose losses as a result of his decision would amount to millions.

Actually, Walker's decision is easy to understand. Edmund Randolph was his close friend. He was the one who had introduced him to Ellen Martin, and he had unfailingly and unflinchingly supported him in every major crisis he had ever experienced. True friendship was sacred, and Walker acted accordingly.

The storm broke at the end of February, 1856, when news of Walker's actions reached New York. In a single day Commodore Vanderbilt lost more than $1 million on the stock market, and his Accessory Transit Company, together with its assets, became worthless.

An angry Commodore Vanderbilt was a man rightly to be feared. Retaliating on many fronts, he sued Walker, Garrison, and Randolph for $1 million and the government of Nicaragua for $500,000. He sent a private emissary to President Rivas and offered him substantial bribes to reverse the seizure.

At the same time he showed his teeth. It so happened —and Garrison apparently had neglected to take this into account—that Vanderbilt had a virtual monopoly of shipping to Nicaragua from both New York and San Francisco. He immediately placed the country under an embargo, and no Vanderbilt steamers went to Nicaraguan ports. Instead, he sent them to Panama, where the overland journey across the Isthmus was shorter.

Still not content, Vanderbilt persuaded the government of Great Britain to seal off Greytown, the principal Nicaraguan port in the Atlantic, because British shareholders in his Transit Company also had suffered. Soon a pair of British gunboats took up positions at the entrance to the Greytown harbor and frightened away any ships that might drop anchor there.

For all practical purposes Nicaragua was cut off from the world. Americans making the coast-to-coast journey by sea were using another route. No more volunteers could reach Walker. All trade was stifled, and the bananas, sugar, and other agricultural products that Nicaragua exported rotted on the docks. Manufactured goods, cloth and even medicines badly needed by the Nicaraguan people were under embargo.

American business and political circles, which had been open in their admiration of William Walker, now regarded him as irresponsible. Few men had much love for Commodore Vanderbilt, but they respected him, and they felt he had been treated unfairly.

The reaction in Great Britain was even stronger. Scores of stockholders in the Accessory Transit Company had lost their entire investment as a result of Walker's capricious act. It must be remembered that the British were deeply involved in Central America, and the government looked at Walker with great apprehension. If he could cancel the charter of one company with impunity and hand its assets to a friend, he could do the same with other investments. Some of Nicaragua's biggest plantations were British-owned and could be expropriated. Even worse, the contagion might well spread to other Central American republics if it remained unchecked. Something had to be done, and quickly.

Walker, the idealistic innocent trapped in the harsh world of power politics, gradually learned of the various steps being taken to hem him in. But he had no notion of the action the British were taking. As an initial move, the War Office in London sent two thousand rifles to Costa Rica, all of them of the latest make and equipped with sights as yet unavailable elsewhere. Accompanying this "gift" was another consisting of one million rounds of ammunition.

Costa Rica, itself anxious to be rid of Walker, asked Britain for naval protection, too. The British replied by sending a cruiser to visit Costa Rica for the purpose of protecting British interests there, and an entire squadron was given the assignment of cruising off the Caribbean coasts of the Central American countries.

Early in March, 1856, President Juan Rafael Mora of Costa Rica announced the mobilization of nine thousand men for the purpose of invading Nicaragua and ridding that country of the "foreign influence under which it has fallen." A few days later a column of Costa Rican troops crossed the border without a declaration of war.

President Rivas of Nicaragua promptly declared war, and in a formal statement he called on the entire civilized world to note that his country was being attacked without provocation.

William Walker also issued a statement, saying that he and his men had come to Nicaragua to fight for democracy and that they continued to pledge themselves to that cause. Walker followed the course urged on him several months earlier by General Maximo

91

Jerez, and urged men of like faith throughout Central America—and specifically in Costa Rica—to join him in his struggle.

His eloquence was so persuasive that Jerez immediately joined the cabinet as Minister of War.

Walker refused to change any of his principles. His American corps was almost one thousand strong, forming a core for his defending army. He refused to accept conscripts, and insisted that he would take only Nicaraguan volunteers. His popularity among the poor of Nicaragua rose even higher, and men flocked to his colors.

His reaffirmation of his faith in democracy, to be sure, offended many of the wealthy Conservatives, who had prospered during the regime of Chamorro. Their support was halfhearted, and many of them privately hoped the Costa Ricans would triumph and return them to power.

The United States government took no position whatever in the matter, preferring to close its eyes and let the force of arms determine the issue. The American public, however, rooted for Walker, and his popularity at home rose to new heights. Ships were chartered in New York and San Francisco, and more recruits came to join him, evading Vanderbilt's embargo.

Bad luck, combined with serious errors in judgment, caused difficulties for Walker from the outset of his military campaign. Epidemics of fever and dysentery spread through his camp, and out of one thousand American troops, four hundred were ill. Most of those who were stricken were his veterans who knew Nicaragua, and only the most recent arrivals seemed immune. Walker himself was incapacitated by a fever, and so were virtually all of his senior officers.

Word was received that the Costa Ricans, several thousand strong, had advanced to the little town of Santa Rosa, south of Lake Nicaragua, and Walker sent six hundred Americans and one thousand Nicaraguans to meet them. If he and his officers had accompanied the expedition the results might have been far different, but Walker gave the command of the force to a man named Louis Schlessinger, who could not have displayed worse judgment.

Schlessinger, a German, spoke a number of languages and had been working for Walker as a diplomat. In that capacity he had enjoyed considerable success, in part because he exuded self-confidence and was clever in his dealings. However, he was completely lacking in military experience, had never fought in a battle, and knew nothing about strategy or tactics.

Not even bothering to send out scouts in order to learn the enemy strength and dispositions, Schlessinger led his sixteen hundred men into certain disaster. They blundered into a Costa Rican trap and found themselves surrounded on three sides, and were badly outnumbered. American recruits and Nicaraguans alike became panicky and fled from the field. One of the first to run away was Schlessinger.

The Costa Ricans closed the trap, and about five hundred of Walker's men, half of them Americans, were slaughtered, their foes giving them no quarter. Granada was stunned when news of the debacle reached the city, and the civilian population became hysterical when it was rumored that Honduras was planning to invade from the north in the immediate future.

Walker left his sickbed and took command of the five hundred Americans who were physically fit. He marched to Rivas, the town where he had suffered his only defeat and, emphasizing the need for strict discipline, prepared for battle against a force of four thousand Costa Ricans.

Before Walker could meet the enemy, he received a frantic message from President Rivas telling him to come to León without delay because the invasion from Honduras had materialized. Walker obeyed and withdrew his men, only to discover that there was no truth to the report.

Before he could turn around again, the Costa Ricans had occupied Rivas and Virgin Bay, seized the Accessory Transit Company's facilities in the latter town, and killed about a dozen American civilian employees. Walker now had no alternative. Unable to wait for Nicaraguan reinforcements, he led his little army of five hundred Americans back to Rivas.

There he launched a surprise attack, killing or wounding almost a thousand of the enemy. His army suffered about a hundred casualties, and he was afraid that his force had been too severely weakened to continue the fight the next day, so he withdrew that night in secret, carrying his wounded with him.

It appeared that the end had come, but the nature of warfare in Central America was even more volatile than Walker realized. The people of Costa Rica had believed their army would sweep unopposed through Nicaragua, but it had suffered heavy casualties, and the country was on the verge of a revolution. President Mora, who had led his troops in person, was forced to hurry home with every man who could march. He left anywhere from one thousand to fifteen hundred sick and wounded behind, and sent a message to Walker asking that they be treated with compassion.

The American veterans, who had seen their own sick

and wounded wantonly murdered by the enemy, eagerly sought revenge, but William Walker would not tolerate such conduct and issued strict orders forbidding reprisals. He returned to Rivas himself, taking every available physician with him, and the Costa Ricans were given medical treatment. As they recovered they were permitted to return unmolested to their own homes across the border.

So Walker's defeat not only was transformed into an unexpected victory, he was also hailed throughout the civilized world as a great humanitarian. Probably no deed he ever performed won him greater popular support in the United States than did his kind treatment of the helpless Costa Ricans. Newspapers throughout the United States lavished praise on him, and even the London press had to admit he had been generous beyond compare.

Costa Rica lost all interest in waging war, Walker's chivalry having won him immediate support in that country. President Mora was so busy trying to repair the damage his campaign had done to his own position at home that he decided to call off his war. He sent Walker a private message in which he indicated that Nicaragua had nothing more to fear from him in the future.

The war fever in Honduras cooled overnight, too, and many people there, particularly the poor, regarded Walker as a hero. Preparations for an invasion were abandoned, and the British warships patrolling the coast were asked to take themselves elsewhere.

Pro-Walker feeling was so strong in the United States that even Commodore Vanderbilt had to appease public opinion with a gesture, and he allowed ships carrying five hundred more American recruits to sail from New

York for Greytown. Members of the Senate and House of Representatives praised the gallant Walker in speech after speech.

William Walker's military reputation had been tarnished, to be sure, and he was no longer regarded as an invincible general. But the people of Nicaragua believed he could do no wrong, and he was more popular there than he had ever been. The Costa Rican invaders had gone home, the Honduran invasion had been abandoned, and the cost had been relatively low. Nicaragua's neighbors had been taught a lesson they would not forget, and by early May, 1856, peace had been restored throughout Central America. Walker had not only succeeded in changing a defeat into a victory, but he had proved he was no freebooter who sought personal gain at the expense of the Nicaraguan people.

In fact, the Conservatives in Granada, who had expected him to take personal possession of large estates and comfortable homes, were astonished by his refusal to claim any benefits for himself. When he was in Granada he used a small room in the Ministry of War building, equipped only with a cot and a small chest of drawers, as a bedchamber, and he conducted his business in a modestly furnished office. Unlike the Central American generals who strutted around in gorgeous uniforms, he wore faded khaki without insignia and at first glance resembled the peasants who cut trails through the jungle for the Transit Company.

He was paid a modest salary equivalent to the wages received by a colonel in the Nicaraguan army, and he refused to accept any other compensation. He would take no gifts from anyone, including the wealthy citizens who hoped to win favors from him, and he would not allow his Americans to take either money or gifts.

Food meant almost nothing to him, and most of his meals consisted of bread, cold meat, and cheese, which he ate in his office. Occasionally he feasted on a melon or a banana.

He accepted few dinner invitations, he worked a minimum of sixteen hours each day, and he never took a day off, saying he could accomplish more on Sundays and holidays, when it was quiet. Long accustomed to seeing Spaniards and Englishmen making themselves wealthy at Nicaraguan expense, the people finally realized, after the abortive Costa Rican invasion, that the man they hailed as their savior sought no material gains of any kind for himself.

Few people realized that William Walker was happier than he had ever been. His secret boyhood dreams had come true. He had won honor and glory, and he was renowned throughout the civilized world. He was the most powerful man in Nicaragua, and his enormous popularity was based on solid achievements.

But it would be a mistake to assume that all of Walker's ambitions had been fulfilled. He had risen so high out of obscurity that he dreamed anew.

7

May 14, 1856, was an important day in the life of William Walker. On that date President Franklin Pierce of the United States, who had previously hesitated for fear of offending Great Britain, finally bowed to public pressure and ordered the State Department to accept the credentials of Father Vijil as Nicaraguan minister. This recognition by Walker's native land was a high point in his career.

Commodore Vanderbilt expressed his anger about it, both publicly and privately, in no uncertain terms. The governments of Costa Rica and Honduras filed official protests with the State Department. Great Britain was displeased and, although in no position to submit a formal diplomatic protest, let her ire be known by sending twenty thousand troops to Canada. American newspapers were filled with speculation over the possibility of a war with Britain.

Meanwhile, in Nicaragua itself, a new crisis was brewing. The cabinet felt that, with the restoration of peace, a new election for President should be held. President Rivas was a candidate to succeed himself, and he was opposed by Maximo Jerez and by Mariano Salazar, one of the country's wealthier men, who had entered the army as a high-ranking officer and whose principal qualification appeared to be his talent as an orator.

There was a fourth, undeclared candidate: William Walker. It is unfair, however, to claim, as some of his earlier biographers did, that he actively sought the position. His popularity was so great in all parts of Nicaragua that the combination of his victory in war and the recognition by the United States would have made it simple for him to take the office by the expedient of declaring himself President.

Certainly all three of the candidates were afraid of him, and the cabinet backtracked, saying that it might be wise to postpone an election until some future time. Rivas also demonstrated a lack of statesmanship by demanding that Walker send half of his Americans home and by refusing to grant them the cash bonuses and homesteads they had been promised.

Walker was displeased. He quietly requested that the election be held without delay, and President Rivas, who was too weak to oppose him, signed the necessary decree. Walker and the main body of his American troops left León and started to march back to Granada, leaving a small detachment in the northern city under the command of Captain von Netzmer.

Trouble erupted almost immediately. Salazar spread an unfounded rumor to the effect that Walker intended to place President Rivas and the entire cabinet under arrest. The President and most cabinet members believed the story and fled to the interior. A mob of peasants and poor urban dwellers, egged on by Salazar, threatened the detachment of Americans, and von Netzmer moved his troops into the cathedral, the most solidly constructed building in the city, for their safety.

Jerez, the Minister of War, who had not fled with the other cabinet members, ordered von Netzmer to evacuate. Uncertain and confused, von Netzmer sent a messenger to Walker, asking for instructions. The reply was rapid and direct: Leave the cathedral and join your comrades. Netzmer and his men caught up with the main American column on the road to Granada.

No one has ever known precisely what happened in the following days. From his jungle hideout President Rivas called Walker a traitor and deposed him as commander in chief of the army. Walker responded with a proclamation deposing Rivas, claiming that the President had invited the troops of Guatemala and El Salvador to invade Nicaragua on his behalf. Whether this charge was accurate or was invented by a less than truthful William Walker has never been determined. If Rivas did request foreign intervention, no proof was produced at the time, and none has ever been unearthed from that day to the present.

What Walker did, in effect, was to follow an old Central American custom by deposing Rivas and naming a Nicaraguan nonentity to serve as provisional President. The election was held on June 29, 1856, and the most that can be said for Walker is that the names of all three of his opponents appeared on the ballot, along with his own. In theory, at least, he gave Rivas, Jerez, and Salazar the opportunity to beat him.

El Nicaraguense, the only newspaper that printed actual figures, declared that 35,000 citizens of the country held the franchise. Of these, Walker's newspaper said, 23,000 voted, and 16,000 of them cast their ballots for the American. These results are suspect. Probably, Walker's enthusiastic supporters, especially in Granada, cheated on his behalf.

Regardless of the chicanery that took place, the outcome of the election was clear. William Walker of Nashville, Tennessee, thirty-two years of age, a former physician, lawyer, and newspaper editor, had been chosen by the people of Nicaragua as their President. At his request, he was inaugurated on July 4, a date that meant nothing to the citizens of Nicaragua.

Virtually all of Granada turned out for the ceremony, and thousands came into the city from the countryside for the festivities, with only the citizens of León and its environs conspicuous by their absence. The army paraded, with the American legion forming the vanguard. Bands played, vendors sold fried plantain and other tropical dishes, and the entire diplomatic corps gathered in front of the cathedral, as did scores of newspaper reporters representing the world press.

Precisely at noon William Walker emerged from the presidential palace and walked alone to the cathedral. He was dressed in a rusty black suit, and American correspondents variously described him as resembling a grocery-store keeper, a Protestant clergyman, and an undertaker.

Most people assumed that Walker would either announce that he was ceding Nicaragua to the United States or offer many special privileges to his native land. Instead, in his inaugural address, he stressed that Nicaragua would maintain her total independence at all costs and would be beholden to no one.

The following day he appointed his cabinet, all of its members Nicaraguans. But he also issued two decrees that marred his popularity. The lesser of them made English the second official language of the country. By far the more important was a law intended to replenish the empty national treasury.

Under this law the property of all citizens who had supported the Costa Rican invasion was forfeited to the government, which was authorized to sell the land, buildings, livestock, and personal belongings of the former owners. Some of the largest and most productive plantations in Nicaragua were included, and the first auction, held in September, 1856, brought in revenues of almost $1 million.

This policy showed Walker at his most insensitive. Real land reform was urgently needed, since a few very wealthy people owned most plantations and ranches, whereas the poor received only token wages. Well-to-do citizens of the United States sent their representatives to bid at the auctions, and most properties were sold to North Americans.

The Nicaraguans felt that Walker had betrayed them. The wealthy who were now landless hated him. The poor discovered their lot was not improved, and found themselves serving foreign instead of domestic masters. Walker's shortsighted land-reform policy may have been his biggest mistake.

That policy also alarmed the governments of the other Central American republics, whose citizens were afraid they would suffer the same fate if Walker expanded his borders. Guatemala and El Salvador, which had not been chastened in the previous war, were especially belligerent, and Great Britain was urging Costa Rica to resume the war.

Walker could hope to survive as President only if he won the unstinting support of the United States, but he was betrayed by his own innocence and lack of experience. He gave his full support to a soldier of fortune from Missouri, Callender Fayssoux, who emplaced several small cannon on a tiny Nicaraguan merchant ship and defied a British warship. Walker forced the captain of the British vessel to apologize, and by humiliating the Royal Navy, the most powerful navy in the world, he made London even more anxious to depose him.

Walker's worst error was his appointment of Domingo de Goicuria, a middle-aged Cuban soldier of fortune, who held the rank of brigadier general in the Nicaraguan army, as his "diplomatic minister at large." At Goicuria's request, Walker gave him a letter, probably written by Goicuria himself, that was to be shown privately to the British government. In it Walker stated that he was unalterably opposed to the annexation of Cuba by the United States. Presumably this curious document was intended to win Britain's friendship.

Goicuria went to the United States before going on to England, but nowhere could he sell the new Nicaraguan bonds, which bore Walker's picture and would pay an interest rate of 6 percent. Americans might admire Walker, but businessmen in New Orleans, St. Louis, Chicago, and New York regarded him as a poor security risk.

Acting completely on his own initiative, Goicuria went to Commodore Vanderbilt and offered him a deal. In return for a loan of a quarter of a million dollars, Goicuria said, Walker would restore the ownership of the Transit Company to the Commodore.

The Commodore agreed, and the delighted Cuban sent off a letter to Granada. But Walker still thought in simple terms, and in his opinion such an arrangement would have constituted a repudiation of his dear friend, Edmund Randolph. He not only rejected the deal, but dismissed Goicuria and revoked his commission in the Nicaraguan army.

Humiliated and angry, Goicuria showed the American newspapers the text of Walker's letter, which had been intended only for the eyes of the British government. The American press exploded, and so did the American people. Walker was branded as a traitor to his native land, a cheap adventurer who was willing to sell out the interests of the United States for his own profit.

Ensuring his own downfall in September, 1856, Walker issued a decree that nullified large portions of the Nicaraguan constitution. It was his intention to reform that document, but his move was universally interpreted as an attempt to revoke the ban on slavery in Nicaragua. In the United States, where the slavery issue dominated political thinking, Walker caused himself great damage in the North. In the South, particularly in New Orleans, prominent citizens began to wonder if it might be a good idea, after all, to buy Walker's bonds.

In Nicaragua the poor were horrified. The Yankee who had become their President intended to sell them into slavery! Nothing Walker could say would convince them otherwise.

The storm was gathering. Guatemala, Honduras, and El Salvador mobilized their troops for an invasion of Nicaragua, and they received arms for that purpose from Great Britain. They were secretly aided by the dissidents of León, including former President Rivas and former War Minister Jerez. Commodore Vanderbilt, smarting after being rebuffed again, tightened his blockade of Nicaraguan ports. Time was running out for the naive William Walker, who knew so little of the ways of the real, practical world.

Costa Rica joined the other Central American republics, and in late September, 1856, they invaded Nicaragua from the north and the south. Great Britain sent a powerful fleet to Greytown in order to cut Walker off from all outside aid.

Walker had only six hundred Americans under arms, and there was no chance that new recruits could join him. He asked for Nicaraguan volunteers, but virtually none appeared. His supplies of food and ammunition were low, and he faced thousands of enemies.

His situation appeared hopeless.

He won a brief respite when a cholera epidemic broke out in the ranks of his foes, forcing them to halt for a time. The campaign was resumed on October 7, and Walker was forced to evacuate the town of Masaya, on the main road to Granada, when a large enemy force threatened to overwhelm him. His disciplined Americans did not panic, however, and pulled out in good order.

Walker retreated toward Granada, but a corps of Guatemalans reached the city first and, after occupying it, indulged in the looting, raping, pillaging, and murder customary in that part of the world.

Newspapers in the United States and Great Britain predicted the imminent collapse of William Walker and his tiny army of American adventurers.

On October 11, however, a miracle occurred. The citizens of Granada, who were being subjected to brutal treatment by their Guatemalan captors, suddenly realized that Walker offered them their only hope of salvation. That night nearly two thousand men, many of them veterans who had served previously with Walker, sneaked out of the city and joined him.

Thus reinforced, Walker attacked the Guatemalans on October 13, routed them, and recaptured Granada.

This success stunned his other foes, who decided they would survive longer at home. The invasion was abandoned, and Walker was restored to power and prestige, with no one to oppose him. The overnight change in his fortunes astonished the world.

The months that followed were peaceful, the most tranquil of Walker's rule, and he made valiant efforts to improve the economy of Nicaragua and make her more secure against her enemies.

His labors were noted by George Law, a tycoon who was trying to wrest control of the Panama shipping trade from Commodore Vanderbilt and who despised Vanderbilt personally. Law conceived the idea of giving massive support to Walker, and winning control of the Accessory Transit Company for himself.

His first move was the hiring of one of the most extraordinary adventurers on earth. Charles Frederick Henningsen was about forty years old, a blond Swedish giant who had fought in a number of European wars and had been a lieutenant under Kossuth in Hungary. He had written two books on military strategy, and by any standards was a professional soldier of high caliber.

Henningsen believed that Walker could drive off the combined might of Nicaragua's neighbors if he had enough artillery, and Law provided him with a large sum of money to purchase what he needed. Henningsen not only bought a number of mortars and howitzers, but he trained volunteers in their use.

The guns and their crews were loaded onto a ship belonging to Law's fleet, and so many men volunteered for the expedition that a second ship had to be outfitted, too. Henningsen even took the precaution of training a company of engineers, men who were capable of building bridges over tropical rivers.

In mid-June, 1857, the ships, both heavily armed, sailed from New York with their load of men, cannon, and ammunition, as well as several thousand rifles of the latest model, which Law was sending to Walker as a gift. No secret was made of Henningsen's departure, but President James Buchanan made no attempt to halt the vessels, and the British, afraid of creating real problems in their relations with the United States, did not dare.

Walker and his veterans greeted the newcomers joyfully, and Henningsen promptly received a commission as major general of the Nicaraguan army, making him the only officer to hold that rank. The two men achieved an immediate rapport, which they maintained until Walker's death.

Henningsen hadn't known what to expect, and he was pleasantly surprised by Walker's legion. These veterans, many bearing the scars of wounds they had suffered in Nicaragua, were superbly disciplined and confident of their own skills. This confidence was justified. Writing about them some years later, Henningsen declared they were the finest marksmen he had ever encountered anywhere.

He was pleased, too, to find that the poor of Nicaragua continued to support President Walker. They had recovered from their fear of enforced slavery and recognized Walker as the one man who, seeking nothing for himself, would preserve their liberties.

Nicaragua's neighbors observed the arrival of Henningsen and his men with great apprehension, and early in July they attacked. Costa Rica sent in a force from the south to take the Accessory Transit Company route, while Guatemala and El Salvador launched an assault from the north, aided by disaffected Nicaraguans from León.

Walker and Henningsen, with 1,000 Americans under

their command, faced the combined forces of about 5,000. The pair acted with dispatch and routed the Costa Ricans from San Juan del Sur. But they had to leave 250 men to guard the Transit route, and that left them only 750 to march north with.

Walker had hoped, as did Henningsen that their artillery would give them the advantage, because they were outnumbered by five to one as they assaulted the foe at Masaya. But the range of their mortars was too short, so they resorted to infantry attacks. The battle raged for three days, and the American sharpshooters took a terrible toll. Lacking reinforcements, the brave little army finally had to withdraw to Granada, where a new epidemic of cholera broke out.

The President of Nicaragua and his major general believed they no longer had a choice. They would have to pull back to Lake Nicaragua to buy time for their men to recuperate, and that meant abandoning Granada to the foe. Walker then made a decision for which he was harshly criticized: rather than allow the capital to fall into the hands of the enemy, he would raze it.

The entire civilian population was evacuated, many of them accompanying Walker and the main American force to the shores of Lake Nicaragua. Henningsen stayed behind with the company of engineers and began the task of systematically blowing up every building in the city. While they were engaged in the work, the Guatemalan invaders reached the city, and the little band took refuge in the cathedral, where a number of refugees had gathered, among them a dozen civilians.

Henningsen proceeded to fight one of his more remarkable battles against the Guatemalans, and with his cannon emplaced on the cathedral steps held the foe at

108

bay while his marksmen decimated the ranks of the attackers.

The invaders' losses were so heavy that they withdrew to regroup, and Henningsen promptly blew up most of the buildings still standing in the heart of the city. Meanwhile, Walker had organized a relief column, and the joint American forces fought with such skill that Henningsen and his men were able to escape, taking the refugees with them.

The Guatemalans had taken such a beating that they withdrew to Masaya, and the Costa Ricans, having had enough of the war, gave up their attempt to take the Transit route and went home. Then the Guatemalans quarreled with the Salvadoreans, and Walker was saved.

His prospects improved still more when a transport bearing new recruits arrived at San Juan del Sur, their landing having been made possible when the Missouri adventurer Fayssoux sank a powerful Costa Rican brig that had challenged his tiny schooner. The new arrivals informed Walker that a much larger group was sailing from New York in the immediate future.

For the rest of the year Walker and his men recuperated.

Commodore Vanderbilt found the situation intolerable. William Walker and a band of a few hundred men were making it impossible for him to regain control of the Accessory Transit Company. The problem, as he saw it with his customary shrewdness, was that Central Americans, regardless of their nationality, were no match for Walker's disciplined marksmen in battle, and they fled from the field whenever they met him in combat. Another way had to be found to defeat him.

The Commodore sent emissaries to meet President Mora of Costa Rica, and soon a plan of action had been organized. With Vanderbilt providing the ships, guns, and ammunition, a large Costa Rican force landed on the Nicaraguan coast and marched inland, capturing the Transit Company's facilities at Virgin Bay before Walker and Henningsen even knew they were in the country. Meantime, a Costa Rican naval force blockaded the main Nicaraguan ports and succeeded in turning away transports carrying four hundred heavily armed volunteers who had come from New Orleans to join Walker.

According to the strategy devised by Vanderbilt's lieutenants, the Guatemalans who still held Masaya would remain there, and would not meet Walker in battle. Instead, they would work in concert with the Costa Ricans and starve him out by blocking all roads and making it impossible for him to receive fresh supplies.

The siege began in December, 1856, and lasted into April, 1857. During that time Walker was virtually sealed off from the outside world, receiving no reinforcements, no ammuniton, and no food. In spite of all the odds against him, he held out, occasionally emerging from his jungle fortress to fight the enemy. On one occasion he defeated the Costa Ricans. In two later battles he battered the Guatemalans, and in one of these engagements fewer than four hundred men routed a force of more than three thousand, an engagement in which the Guatemalans left more than seven hundred dead on the field.

Walker continued to hope for new miracles, but time worked for his foes. His men were reduced to eating mule meat, and many of them, particularly the new arrivals, chafed under Walker's discipline and the difficult living conditions. They began to wonder why they were starving, and Walker's only answer was that they would be murdered if they surrendered.

The wily President Mora of Costa Rica delivered the final blow, one that neither he nor his alies, even now, could achieve by force of arms. In mid-April of 1857 the sentries manning the American jungle outposts were pelted with leaflets crudely printed in English.

Any American who surrendered, Mora promised, would be treated honorably. He would be given food and liquor, and women would be provided for him. He would not be harmed or held prisoner, but would be given free transportation back to the United States.

Walker, himself a scarecrow, delivered a series of impassioned speeches, but he could not stem the tide of desertion. Men who wore rags, who were starving, who were plagued by the mosquitoes and spiders and snakes of the Nicaraguan jungle were deaf to talk of honor. They had learned that glory was empty, and the cause of President Walker was no longer sacred to them.

Singly and in pairs, sometimes in threes and fours, they crept out of the jungle at night. There was only one way Walker could halt them. Calling together the members of his shrunken army, he announced that he would freely permit any man who wanted to leave to walk unmolested out of his camp. The desertions were stopped.

Walker did not know it, but both the Costa Ricans and the Guatemalans were suffering from cholera, so their own positions were tenuous.

At the same time, Commodore Vanderbilt discovered that those who played with fire could be burned. The Costa Ricans who had captured the Accessory Tansit Company's installations on his behalf had no intention of turning them over to him.

Vanderbilt prodded the United States government, and President Buchanan, a cautious procrastinator by nature, realized that something had to be done. He was worried about the effect on American public opinion if he allowed Walker and his men to perish in the jungle, so he sent a United States Navy squadron to Central America. The overall commander was Commodore Hiram Paulding, who was aboard his flagship, the frigate *Wabash*. The sloop of war *St. Mary's*, under Commander Charles N. Davis, sailed on to San Juan del Sur, and Davis carried instructions to end the war by any means possible.

Davis' first step was to confer with President Mora of Costa Rica, who saw an opportunity to be rid of William Walker. He agreed to give the Americans safe conduct out of the jungle and allow them to leave the country, but as a condition of this arrangement he insisted that all American artillery be turned over to him.

Davis sent several junior officers inland, carrying a letter to Walker under a flag of truce. The United States was willing to evacuate the entire force, Davis said, but Walker first would have to work out an armistice with Mora.

The angry Walker was trapped. He knew nothing about the cholera that was making such inroads in the enemy ranks, and he felt he and his men could not hold out much longer.

Late in April two of Mora's emissaries held a meeting with Walker, and the peace terms were arranged. Walker was adamant on one point: the Nicaraguans serving under his command had to be allowed to return in peace to their homes, unmolested, with guarantees that no reprisals would be taken against them in the future.

The Costa Ricans reluctantly agreed.

Walker had no intention of allowing his enemies to use the valuable mortars and howitzers he had been hoarding. Nothing in the agreement specified they had to be in working order, so on April 30 Henningsen and his engineers spiked the guns and blew up their ammunition.

On May 1 Walker delivered a farewell address to his little army. He thanked them for their services, praised them for their valor, and assured them that history would never forget them. Then he told them they would have to part company for a time. He and his staff would go to San Juan del Sur, where they would board the *St. Mary's*. The bulk of the army would travel by the Transit route to Greytown, where the *Wabash* awaited them.

The newer members of the expedition failed to realize that Walker had been given no voice in these arrangements, and believed he was deserting them. On the journey to Greytown they were robbed by Costa Ricans of most of their belongings, and the newspapermen who awaited them with the American squadron reported that they resembled filthy scarecrows when they boarded the flagship.

Walker's troubles were not yet over. When he reached the *St. Mary's*, Commander Davis insisted that he turn over his schooner, the *Granada*, to the United States. He and Fayssoux refused until the Commander threatened to sink the little ship. Only then did they comply, and both were outraged when Davis handed the vessel over to the Costa Ricans. They were only partly mollified when, thanks to inept seamanship, the Costa Rican boarding party rammed the ship into rocks on the shore and sank her.

Davis had the courtesy to receive Walker with full

military honors. He provided him with a private cabin and, immediately after sailing, gave a dinner in his honor. Davis was impressed by the loyalty Walker's officers showed him, and by the dignity displayed by the little man who had made history in Central America.

Nothing in Walker's manner indicated tht he had suffered a severe defeat and that he had been fortunate to escape with his life. His meteoric career appeared to be ended, but he seemed to regard the fate that had overtaken him as a temporary, unpleasant interlude, and if he was not serene, at least he was not particularly disturbed.

The best guide to Walker's military accomplishments is Henningsen. He wrote that, in all, approximately 2,-500 to 2,800 Americans served under Walker in Nicaragua at one time or another. Of these, no more than 1,000 ever fought with him in a single engagement. Because of illness and other problems, the actual number may have been no more than 800 at any one time. Approximately 1,000 Americans had died of wounds or illness; 700 had deserted, many of them in the final campaign; and about 250 had been honorably discharged, many because their wounds had made it impossible for them to continue their military careers. A total of 80 had been captured by the enemy, and their fate was unknown. They were presumed to have been murdered.

On the other hand, Walker's foes, including the forces of the other Central American republics and the small number from León who had faced him in his last campaign numbered from 17,500 to 20,000 men, approximately 6,000 of whom had been killed or wounded in battle. Henningsen also wrote that it was impossible for him to estimate how many of Walker's Central

114

American foes had died of cholera, yellow fever, and other diseases, but a guess of 5,000 would not be high.

In retrospect, William Walker was guilty of blatant interference in the lives of other men. Certainly he must bear at least a measure of the responsibility for the residue of hatred toward North Americans and Europeans that persists in the Spanish-speaking republics of Central America down to the present day.

But Walker was unique in one respect. The others, from Commodore Vanderbilt and the English financiers to the military adventurers, regarded Central America as a happy hunting ground for plunder and exploitation. Without exception they hoped to make themselves wealthy—or wealthier—at the expense of the people of small, poor nations that were unable to protect themselves from powerful marauders.

Walker, however, had no desire for personal financial gain. It is true that he sought glory for himself, and in that respect he succeeded. But his interest in the welfare of the people of Central America was genuine, and during his brief career as President of Nicaragua he made a sincere effort to improve the lot of the poor. His methods were crude and his land-reform program was a nightmare that accomplished nothing for anyone, but this was due, at least in part, to his complete lack of experience in government and his failure to understand the principles of economics.

Many generations would pass before concerted efforts would be made in Central America to obtain land reforms that would enable the poor to earn a living beyond the basic subsistence level. Those efforts continue down to the present day. William Walker must be given credit for being the first to think in such terms, and if his attempts to help the hungry masses were clumsy and misguided, at least his heart was in the right place. That was why the wealthy dictators and their supporters in the other Central American nations hated him and banded together to destroy him.

Long after Walker was forgotten in his own country, he was remembered in Central America. His exploits were exaggerated, as were the principles he attempted to espouse, and the poor in Nicaragua and other countries came to think of him as he liked to think of himself, as the proverbial knight on a white charger, the selfless hero who sought only the good of others and cared nothing about himself.

8

On the morning of May 27, 1857, the sloop of war *St. Mary's* docked at New Orleans, and a crowd of "many thousands," according to the local newspapers, was on hand to greet the returning William Walker. The police set up a cordon to protect him, but his enthusiastic admirers broke through the lines. An open carriage was provided, the team of horses was uncoupled, and men pulled the hero through the streets to the St. Charles Hotel, the best in the city, where a large suite awaited him.

More thousands gathered in the street outside, and Walker was obliged to appear on a balcony and make a short speech of thanks. The crowd refused to disperse until he had made four or five such appearances.

President Buchanan had ordered that no charges be brought against Walker for his violations of the neutrality laws, so he was a free man. His personal funds were limited, but admirers paid his hotel bill and, it appears, supplied him with all the ready cash he needed.

On May 29 a mass meeting was organized on his behalf, and a crowd of about ten thousand came to honor him. Walker gave an extemporaneous address that lasted the better part of two hours, and was cheered repeatedly. Some of his statements were remarkably blunt. He said he had received no support from the Administration of former President Pierce. He openly blamed Commodore Vanderbilt for many of his troubles, and he was equally candid in ascribing some of his woes to the government of Great Britain.

Walker also said he had received no support from President Buchanan in the few months of his presidency. But he displayed tact in mentioning the new Chief Executive, and revealed that he had received an invitation that very day to come to Washington for a conference with Buchanan on Central America.

According to the newspaper stories of his address, Walker also made no secret of the fact that he considered his work in Central America unfinished and that he intended to return to Nicaragua as soon as he could make the necessary arrangements.

Leaving New Orleans, he traveled to Washington by easy stages, and everywhere he was given a hero's welcome. His parents were no longer living, but a huge reception was held for him in Nashville. He visited his sister, Alice Walker Richardson, in Louisville, and the press there devoted many columns to him. In Cincinnati he was given the keys to the city, and a parade was held in his honor.

Washington was accustomed to celebrities, and its welcome was more subdued. Walker was received at the White House as a private American citizen rather than as the former head of a foreign state. He spent more than three hours conferring with the President in private. No record was kept of the conversation, and neither the President nor Walker made any statement after the meeting.

Walker subsequently asserted that he told Buchanan of his intention to return to Nicaragua, and said that the President encouraged him. Members of the Administration later denied this allegation, claiming that Walker had fabricated the whole story.

What probably happened was that the President showed sympathy toward the man who had become a national hero. Buchanan, as a former Senator from Pennsylvania, ambassador, and Secretary of State, had developed a subtle approach to visitors. Frequently he smiled, nodded, and seemed to encourage them, but it later proved impossible for anyone to quote him directly. He used hints as a fine art, so it is likely that Walker actually believed the President intended to support him.

From Washington Walker went on to New York, where the public acclaim dwarfed the receptions given for him elsewhere. He was escorted into the city by an honor guard, and was paraded from the Battery through the Wall Street district, with thousands on hand to cheer him. An enormous crowd awaited him at his hotel, and for days people by the thousands stood outside, hoping to catch a glimpse of him.

He was the guest of General and Mrs. Henningsen at Wallack's Theatre, and the audience there wouldn't stop cheering until he made a speech. Brass bands serenaded him from the street outside his hotel, and crowds followed him everywhere. The press was always at his heels.

After three days and nights of hero worship Walker could tolerate no more, and he went into hiding at the Manhattan home of a supporter. There, with General Henningsen and Colonel Hornsby acting as his principal aides, he got down to the business he had been planning with great care.

Walker held a series of meetings attended by the officers who had served under him in Nicaragua. All were completely loyal to him, and he knew he could trust them without reservation. Together they formed an organization, which they called the Central American League. Its purpose was to raise funds, purchase supplies, and enlist recruits for a new voyage to Nicaragua.

Thanks to a quirk of coincidental timing, the frigate *Wabash* reached New York from Nicaragua while Walker was still in the city. On board were about 150 of the veterans who had endured the four-month jungle siege with him, and the refugees also included several American women and children.

A number of the veterans still believed Walker had deserted them, and in interviews with the press they made no secret of their hatred toward him. Anything that touched on Walker was news, and the newspapers gave considerable space to their anti-hero sentiments, but whether these views actually tarnished his image is difficult to determine.

Walker's lieutenants scattered, each taking responsibility for fund raising and recruiting in a different section of the United States. General Henningsen was in charge of New York, and Colonel Hornsby was sent to San Francisco. All members of the group were highly optimistic.

Had they been economists or practical politicians they would have known better. The United States was in the grip of what later came to be known as the recession of 1857. The stock market collapsed, and many thousands were unemployed. The general feeling of unrest this caused increased as word came out of Kansas concerning the bloody, continuing fighting there between proslavery and antislavery adherents. The United

120

States was drifting toward civil war, and although people in many parts of the country admired William Walker, the times were too uncertain for many men of means to give him substantial public support.

Walker himself quietly returned to New Orleans, and went into hiding there so he could pursue his business out of the public eye. As usual, he was his own most effective fund raiser, and he obtained enough money for one of his agents to purchase a brig, the *Fashion*. His name did not appear in the transaction; presumably the ship would be used to carry cargo between American ports.

The slavery question that was tearing the United States apart occupied all of President Buchanan's time and energy, and he wanted no new filibustering expeditions that might harm America's relations with Great Britain or cause new problems in the Central American republics. He instructed Secretary of State Lewis Cass, who had previously shown sympathy for William Walker, to enforce the neutrality laws.

On November 10, federal marshals appeared at the New Orleans house in which Walker was staying and placed him under arrest. The supplies already stored in the hold of the *Fashion* were of the sort needed for military expedition, but the federal prosecutor could not prove that Walker intended to sail the ship to Nicaragua. Therefore, Walker was placed on bail of $2,000 pending a trial and then released.

Walker immediately put into operation a secret plan that had been prepared for just such an emergency. Blithely ignoring the fact that he was on bail and was not supposed to travel, he and his principal lieutenants—including Hornsby, Fayssoux, Anderson, and Netzmer—boarded a mail boat sailing from New Orleans to

121

Mobile. At each of the boat's many stops they were joined by groups of men who had previously left New Orleans in accordance with a prearranged schedule. Others traveled directly to Mobile.

No attempt had been made by the federal court to impound the *Fashion,* so she was allowed to sail quietly from New Orleans. The authorities must have known Walker's intentions, but he was still so highly regarded in New Orleans that officials quietly looked the other way.

The *Fashion* appeared a few days later in the outer portion of Mobile Bay, where she took on large quantities of arms, ammunition, and additional supplies. If New Orleans liked Walker, Mobile positively worshiped him, and virtually the whole city became party to a conspiracy.

When Walker, his lieutenants, and a large number of healthy, vigorous young men appeared in the city, no one noticed them, and they might have been invisible as they had themselves rowed out to the *Fashion.* Other young men went by boat to the brig in separate groups, and no one bothered to question them.

Finally the federal authorities in Mobile went out to the *Fashion* to conduct a formal inspection. These gentlemen did not see Walker or the 270 men who accompanied him. They also saw no arms, no ammunition, and no supplies. The ship was declared harmless and was given the right to leave port for her destination, regardless of whether it was domestic or foreign.

Although the federal officials in Mobile were closing their eyes to Walker's activities, the President changed his mind. Buchanan was making a serious attempt to improve American relations with Great Britain, and William Walker was a perfect scapegoat. Newspapers had printed the story that the *Fashion* had sailed from Mobile, presumably headed for Nicaragua, and the President issued a highly publicized order to the Navy. It was imperative, he declared, that the brig be intercepted and escorted back to the United States.

A few days later Buchanan sent a message to Congress on a number of subjects, and in it he attacked Walker with great vigor. Outrages such as those Walker had committed previously in Central America, he said, would never again be tolerated because they did the United States no good and would "injure its interests."

Secretary of the Navy Isaac Toucey, who may have sympathized with Walker, issued an order to the Navy's Caribbean squadron in vague wording that made it difficult, if not impossible, to intercept the *Fashion.*

Meanwhile, Walker happily drilled his men on board the brig and spent his spare time writing articles for *El Nicaraguense.* Through no accident he carried his printer with him, and in the hold of the ship were new presses.

Walker knew precisely what he was doing. His first objective was the capture of the key to the Transit Company's operations, Fort Castillo, which stood at the junction of Lake Nicaragua and the San Juan River, which emptied into the harbor at Greytown. In the harbor the *U.S.S. Saratoga,* a heavily armed frigate, stood guard to prevent Walker from landing, so he used his knowledge of Nicaraguan geography to perpetrate a trick.

Another river, the Colorado, which was a tributary of the San Juan, also emptied into the sea, and its mouth was unguarded. Walker landed a heavily armed party under Colonel Anderson at the mouth of the Colorado, then blithely sailed on to Greytown. Challenged by the *Saratoga,* he pretended the *Fashion* was a merchant ship landing passengers who intended to cross Nicaragua via the Transit Company's facilities.

Too late the captain of the *Saratoga* realized his error, and by this time Walker's entire company had gone ashore. In order to avoid trouble with the United States Navy, Walker moved his camp a short distance inland on the San Juan River and awaited word from Anderson.

Twelve days passed before he finally heard from his subordinate. The reliable Anderson had achieved complete success, capturing the river steamers and taking Fort Castillo from the Costa Ricans without the loss of a single man. His messenger said he was following with his main body, and would be joining Walker in a few days.

Meanwhile, a British mail steamer carried word of the *Saratoga*'s humiliation to Commodore Paulding on board the *Wabash*, which was in Panamanian waters. Paulding immediately sailed north with a strong squadron, which included another frigate, the *Fulton*.

Reaching Greytown, Paulding apprised himself of the situation and took prompt action. First, he sent a battalion of Marines, three hundred strong, to occupy a position inland of Walker's camp on the San Juan River. Then he sent Walker a succinct message.

Paulding demanded the immediate, unconditional surrender of Walker and his entire company, and said that unless his order was obeyed immediately, he would order his Marines to attack. At the same time, he said, he would bombard Walker's camp with the more than two hundred naval cannon he carried on the ships of his squadron.

William Walker was courageous but not foolish enough to challenge the armed might of the powerful

124

United States Navy squadron. "I surrender to the United States," he said, and led his men into Greytown.

Many who saw him later commented on his extraordinary dignity. Not until he reached the privacy of Commodore Paulding's quarters on board the *Wabash* did he break down and weep.

Walker and company were returned to New York.

Supporters who included prominent attorneys, political leaders, and even high-ranking army officers accompanied him when he went to the office of the United States marshal, Isaiah Rynders, and volunteered to have himself placed in custody. Rynders, who happened to be one of his great admirers, refused to arrest him, saying no warrant had been issued for the purpose. They agreed to go to Washington together, voluntarily, for a showdown.

Before they departed, Walker addressed a crowded press conference, and he pulled no punches. Commodore Paulding, he declared, had vastly exceeded his authority by invading the territory of a friendly nation and, using the threat of force, had kidnapped 270 men and returned them to the United States. The flag of Nicaragua had been insulted, Walker said, and a grievous error had been committed. The wrong could be righted only by returning him and his company to the place where they had been apprehended, and by giving back to him all of the property that had been confiscated.

The incident created a furor. Mass meetings were held in many American cities denouncing Commodore Paulding's conduct and the order sent by the President to the Secretary of the Navy that had precipitated the crisis. A bill was introduced in the House of Representatives authorizing the payment of indemnity to Walker for the wrongs that the government had done him.

Walker arrived in Washington amid great fanfare on December 27, 1857. A deeply embarrassed President Buchanan tried to ignore him, but Walker made that impossible by writing him a long letter and making it public.

He was the President-in-exile of a friendly nation, he declared, and he expressed deep contempt for Paulding's actions.

Buchanan, as usual, temporized.

On January 4, 1858, the Senate passed a resolution requesting that it be given all documents pertaining to the controversy, and Buchanan could no longer remain silent. He addressed a communication to the Senate in which he once again demonstrated his extraordinary ability to walk a tightrope gracefully. Commodore Paulding, he wrote, had "committed a grave error." But "this was done from pure and patriotic motives." Predicting that the interests of the United States would be greatly expanded in Central America in the years ahead, he nevertheless vaguely condemned what he called "lawless military expeditions" in the area that had originated in the United States.

The President's message was a signal that unleashed torrents of debate in both the Senate and the House. Walker was praised and condemned; Paulding was attacked and defended. The slavery controversy was forgotten for the moment, and so was all other business pending before the Congress. Fifteen senators made long speeches in which every aspect of the case was brought to light, and every phase of Walker's career was examined with care. From January 8 to January 15 no other business came before the Senate and only minor matters came to the attention of the House. At least ten different resolutions were introduced in the Senate on the case, many of them conflicting.

It appeared that William Walker had caused the business of the United States government to grind to a halt.

On January 16 several leaders of the Senate and House called at the White House, and a compromise was reached with the President. All resolutions pending in both houses of Congress were dropped. The Secretary of the Navy publicly but mildly censured Commodore Paulding and temporarily relieved him of his command. No legal action was taken against Walker, and all charges against him were dropped. The President and his Administration continued to oppose Walker, but many members of the Senate and House supported him. Nothing was done to restore the property that had been taken from him.

Walker had received a setback, but had won something of a moral victory. Certainly at this time he was the most famous man in the United States.

Leaving Washington in mid-January, he traveled south, and his journey became a triumphal tour. The antislavery editorials he had written as a young editor in New Orleans were forgotten, and his attempts to change the constitution of Nicaragua were regarded anew as proof that he supported the institution of slavery, even though he had done nothing in Nicaragua to warrant that assumption.

The real reason the South hailed him is not difficult to understand. The slaveholding states constituted a minority that chafed under the various restrictions placed on them by the free states of the North. Walker, himself a Southerner by birth and by long association, was one individual who refused to be bound by federal laws and who thumbed his nose at the federal government.

Thousands turned out to greet him in Richmond, and a dinner was given in his honor. The same thing happened in Montgomery. In Mobile he delivered an address to a huge throng, and he indicated that he was returning to New Orleans to fight his case in the courts. He also revealed that President Buchanan was secretly sponsoring a filibustering expedition into Mexico, and that General Henningsen had gone there to lead an illegal army.

This news was a new bombshell. It happened to be the truth, but the embarrassed President denied it. The North believed him, but the South preferred to take Walker's word.

The Alabama Legislature promptly granted a charter to the Mobile and Nicaragua Steamship Company, which some of Walker's supporters had founded in his behalf. The Central American League was reorganized and revived under a new name, the Southern Emigration Society. Walker's lieutenants began anew the task of raising funds and finding recruits for a new invasion of Nicaragua.

Walker himself embarked on a lecture tour that took him to all parts of the South through the better part of 1858. These speeches, undertaken principally to raise funds, indicated that a deep-rooted change had taken place in his personality. Walker was now thirty-four years old, and he had gone through physical suffering in Nicaragua. What he regarded as persecution by the federal government had made him hard and cynical, and that bitterness was reflected in every speech he made.

His high-minded idealism had vanished, and so had

his sense of humor. He attacked the administration of President Buchanan repeatedly, and no longer even mentioned his dedication to the principles of democracy. Instead he based his position on legality. He was the legally elected President of the Republic of Nicaragua, and meddlers who hated him were preventing him from fulfilling his destiny. The Manifest Destiny of the United States no longer interested him; his one concern now was the personal destiny of General William Walker, President-in-exile of Nicaragua.

In September, 1858, his case finally came to trial in New Orleans. Several attorneys represented him, but in effect Walker really acted in his own defense. He attacked the neutrality laws, condemned President Buchanan, reviewed the actions Commodore Paulding had taken against him and, in all, reminded the entire nation of events the Administration would have preferred to forget.

Never had Walker been more vitriolic, more forceful, more blunt. Never had he been so unyielding in demanding what he regarded as his rights. He refused to compromise, and he insisted that he would achieve his ultimate triumph, no matter what the odds against him were. His faith in his destiny as the leader of a small Central American country was unshaken. His speeches to the jury, and he made many, indicate that he had become a man possessed by inner demons that were driving him toward the one goal that mattered to him, regardless of the cost.

There can be little doubt that Walker had lost whatever sense of perspective he had possessed. He was still a filibuster, still a soldier of fortune, but whatever joy he had felt in earlier years had disappeared from his nature. He was a lost soul now, a sad swashbuckler determined to rule Nicaragua or to die in the attempt.

The jury was split. Ten members voted for the acquittal of the defendant and two found him guilty.

Walker wanted total exoneration, and demanded another trial.

But the federal government was weary of the prosecution, and the district attorney announced that all charges would be dropped.

Newspaper reporters surrounded Walker as he left the courtroom, and he informed them, with his customary bluntness, that he would return to Nicaragua. His cause would triumph, he said, and he would eat Christmas dinner in Granada.

9

President Buchanan knew that William Walker would make another attempt to disturb the peace of Central America, and in so doing would again disturb the relations between the United States and Great Britain. In order to draw the filibuster's teeth he put into action a plan of his own.

A onetime associate of Commodore Vanderbilt, Joseph L. White, was awarded the virtually defunct charter of an organization known as the Atlantic and Pacific Ship Canal Company. The one advantage of the maneuver was that this organization had been the first to be granted transit rights by Nicaragua. Buchanan promptly recognized the claims of White's reconstituted company, and he notified the British government that London's rights would be protected, too. Commodore Vanderbilt's claims were ignored, and so was the existence of William Walker.

Showing the usual disdain of large powers for the rights of small nations in administering their affairs as they thought best for themselves, the United States and Great Britain automatically assumed that Costa Rica, which controlled the Transit route, and Nicaragua, on whose soil the route lay, would concur in the decision made by Washington and London.

Nicaragua and Costa Rica did nothing of the kind. Walker's successor as President of Nicaragua, Tomás Martínez, was a wealthy Conservative who dreaded the day the filibuster would return. President Mora of Costa Rica wanted to ensure that Walker kept his distance, too. Both men believed they could accomplish this goal by accumulating enough money to maintain large armies.

At this juncture, while President Buchanan was working with White, a Parisian named Felix Belly came to Central America. He represented a French syndicate, and on behalf of his colleagues he asked for the Nicaraguan transit rights. In return he offered something to Nicaragua and Costa Rica that had not occurred to the United States and Great Britain: a large share of the new company's rights. This meant that the two Central American countries would earn considerably more than half of the profits.

They accepted the offer.

The President of the United States, the Congress, and the American press were very angry. Much was said about the violation of the Monroe Doctrine by France. Nothing was said about the basic right of Nicaragua and Costa Rica to act as sovereign states and to earn a share in the profits of a company that used their soil and manpower.

In spite of the diplomatic furor raised in the summer of 1858, nothing much happened. Suddenly, for complicated domestic reasons, the French Emperor, Napoleon III, disavowed the whole thing.

The question of the transit right came alive again. This time President Buchanan favored the cause of

Commodore Vanderbilt. The wily financier did nothing, but said vaguely that the physical properties of the Accessory Transit Company had deteriorated and that large sums would be needed to make the route operable again. In the autumn of 1858, roughly at the time of William Walker's trial in New Orleans, the truth of the matter finally emerged in the United States Senate. It was revealed that Vanderbilt was being paid approximately $500,000 per year by the shipping lines that sailed to Panama in both the Atlantic and Pacific. In return he had agreed to do nothing to put the Nicaraguan transit back on its feet.

Suddenly, it appeared, the overland route of passengers through Nicaragua had become worthless. Panama had won the sweepstakes, and although members of Congress could protest all they pleased, no one could force Vanderbilt to renew the Nicaraguan crossing, especially when he was being paid a handsome sum not to do so.

Vanderbilt had washed his hands of Nicaragua. He was busy building and acquiring railroads, as well as establishing a transatlantic steamship service, and he had already grasped what others were just beginning to learn—that the Nicaraguan transit had lost its value. Passengers traveling between the Eastern seaboard of the United States and California had discovered that the journey across the Isthmus of Panama was much shorter and less arduous than the Nicaraguan transfer. So, even if more money were poured into equipment to make the facilities of the Accessory Transit Company safer and more comfortable, it could never recapture the lion's share of the business it had once commanded.

President Martínez of Nicaragua, still looking over his shoulder at the ghost of William Walker, realized late in 1858 that the major powers no longer had a reason for wanting him to maintain a stable government. He appealed to Great Britain for help and support and received both, in return for which he granted the British valuable mining rights, shipping concessions, and other prerogatives that increased their stake in Nicaragua.

This treaty made it impossible for Walker to return to Nicaragua. British warships would either capture his expedition at sea or bombard him if he managed to reach Greytown. British troops would pursue him ashore.

Never daunted, he came up with a new scheme in the late autumn of 1858. A revolution was brewing in Honduras, its core being a party also known as Liberals, who had been friends and allies of the old Liberals in Nicaragua with whom Walker had first cast his lot there.

So he would go to Honduras. There he would help the Liberals to achieve power, and then, having established a solid base, march overland into Nicaragua.

His trial had won him so much support that he had no difficulty in recruiting a force of three hundred men or in chartering a ship for the alleged purpose of "peaceful migration to Nicaragua." He and his followers went to Mobile, intending to sail in mid-December.

But President Buchanan's patience had been tried long enough, and federal officials in Mobile were under strict orders not to allow Walker to sail. His ship was seized, and he was called before a federal grand jury to face charges of conspiracy to evade the law.

The jurors were sympathetic to Walker's cause and refused to indict him, but his victory was short-lived. United States marshals had dispersed his little army and had, where necessary, forced its members to return to their own homes. The cargo of arms, ammunition, and military supplies was confiscated, and the owners of the ship, fearing the vessel would be sent to the bottom of the Caribbean by the Royal Navy, revoked Walker's charter.

Overnight William Walker became a pathetic figure, a hero without a cause.

In his own mind, however, he could not give up. The growing controversy over the slavery question left him cold, and he had no interest in it. He had become obsessed with the urgent desire to conquer Central America.

Within a few days he and his faithful lieutenants rounded up a band of about one hundred men, most of them drifters and alcoholics from the Mobile waterfront. Through the valiant efforts of a few loyal supporters, he obtained a small vessel, the *Susan,* and although denied the right to leave Mobile he defied the authorities and sailed late at night.

His little expedition lacked sufficient arms, ammunition, food, medicines, or other supplies. Walker was blindly, stupidly pursuing his destiny, and even if he had been able to reach his destination it is doubtful that the men who had accompanied him could have fought a battle.

The *Susan* never reached Honduras. The ship was halted in the Caribbean by a squadron of Royal Navy warships. The company was taken on board one of them and, with due ceremony, returned to Mobile.

The citizens of Mobile gave a series of dinners and balls in honor of the officers of the Royal Navy squadron. The fact that they had apprehended William Walker, until recently the toast of the South, was largely ignored.

By this time the city had lost interest in Walker. Many men in the United States and abroad now regarded war between the states as inevitable, and Great Britain openly favored the cause of the South. The British economy was largely dependent on mills that produced cloth, and most of the cotton imported into England for manufacture came from the South. This natural affinity created a close bond.

Some of Walker's early biographers were puzzled by his refusal to take part in the growing fight over the slavery question, in which he had shown such interest in his youth. But he now regarded it as a question that concerned others, not himself, and it left him untouched.

He had been a nonentity until he went to Central America, and there he had achieved fame great renown and power. His thirst for both was insatiable. It is safe to say that a yearning for military ventures and adventure for its own sake no longer attracted him. He regarded himself as the savior of Central America in general and of Nicaragua in particular. Granada was his capital, his real home, and he was the head of what he believed to have been the last legitimate government of Nicaragua. Nothing could keep him from returning.

Money was increasingly difficult to obtain. Patriots in both the North and the South now preferred to stay at home, where they felt increasingly certain they would be called to fight for principles in which they believed. All over the United States, especially in the South, arsenals were being stocked with rifles, gunpowder, and ammunition.

The day of the filibuster was at an end, but Walker either did not know it or refused to believe it. He intended to let nothing prevent his return to Nicaragua.

136

In all this he was still supported by General Henningsen, who had not lost his own taste for adventure, and together they concocted yet another plan. George Law, the financier, was still interested in gaining control of the Nicaraguan transfer, and agreed to help.

According to this ingenious scheme, Law would provide a steamer large enough to accommodate one hundred men, and he would file for permission to sail to Panama. Not only did the federal government have no right to prevent such a sailing, but proof would be provided that another vessel would be waiting for the men in the Pacific after they had crossed the Isthmus by the overland route, and would transport them to California. In actuality, however this ship would sail only as far as the Pacific coast of Nicaragua and deposit them there. There were few British warships in the Pacific, if any, so the odds were great that the landing would be made without interference.

Walker ostensibly would have no connection with this voyage. He would leave the United States separately and go to Havana, where the steamer would pick him up en route to Panama.

The plan seemed foolproof. For better or worse, however, Walker was the victim of unexpected publicity. Accompanied only by von Netzmer, he carried out the first stage of the plan by sailing from New Orleans to Havana, but his departure was noted by a reporter for the leading local newspaper, the *Picayune*. The paper published a story to the effect that Walker was going to California by way of Panama, and that he hoped to organize a new Nicaraguan expedition in San Francisco.

Besieged by newsmen when he reached Cuba, Walker protested that he intended to sail on to Europe in order to obtain backing there. This story was so thin that the

137

federal authorities in New Orleans suspected the truth, seized the steamer, and dispersed the company, which included Walker's usual loyal lieutenants.

When Walker learned of the expedition's collapse he and von Netzmer quickly returned to New Orleans. He was determined to try again, and he went to New York, where he and General Henningsen persuaded Law to support one more venture.

This scheme was the most complicated and grandiose that had yet been devised. One of Law's steamers, the *Philadelphia*, was equipped with a large secret hold, and quantities of arms and ammunition were stored there. The vessel then sailed from New York to New Orleans to pick up "passengers" for Panama. Included in this company of 150 people, as it happened, were Walker and his principal aides.

In the meantime a second Law ship, the *St. Louis*, would sail directly from New York at the appropriate time, carrying an additional 200 volunteers. The two groups would meet in Panama, cross the Isthmus together, and then be transported to the Pacific shores of Nicaragua by a third Law steamer.

At first all went well. The federal authorities in New Orleans inspected the *Philadelphia* and did not find the arms and munitions. Then apparently someone talked out of turn; no one, down to the present day, has ever discovered how the government learned of the scheme. Navy gunboats were ordered to halt the ship in the Mississippi River delta. There a company of United States Army troops went on board, and more thorough inspection was made. This time the arms and ammunition were found.

A telegram alerted federal authorities in New York, and the *St. Louis* was seized shortly before her scheduled sailing. Once again the volunteers were dispersed. Law, who had spent large sums of money in vain, became discouraged and refused to help again. William Walker had come to the end of the road. Or so it seemed.

What is remarkable is that he still retained the loyalty of his principal lieutenants. Men like Henningsen, Hornsby, Anderson, von Netzmer, and Fayssoux stood by him through one disappointment after another and were willing to follow wherever he wanted to lead them. It must be stressed that these men were not naive idealists. They knew, certainly, that even if Walker succeeded in regaining power in Nicaragua they would not become wealthy, but would serve simply as the commanders of his American legion.

By the latter part of September, 1859, when Walker's newest scheme collapsed, civil war seemed inevitable, and as professional soldiers, long experienced in leading men into battle, these officers might have had ample opportunity to fight again for either the Union or the Confederacy. Instead they chose to remain blindly, stubbornly loyal to William Walker. Why? There is no definitive reason; one can only assume that his leadership was so dynamic that those who knew him best continued to cling to him, no matter how great the repeated disappointments they suffered.

But even Walker's lieutenants could do nothing for him after his latest expedition had been thwarted. No financial support could be found anywhere, and Walker was back where he started, a man without a penny in his pocket, no concrete hopes, and no way to earn a living.

At this critical time in his life a Mobile publisher came to Walker and asked him to write a book about his experiences in Central America. *The War in Nicaragua* was the result, and Walker wrote it in a very few months.

Of all his exploits the book may be the most remarkable, although it makes difficult reading.

In a volume of more than four hundred pages Walker maintained an astonishing objectivity. He referred to himself in the third person throughout the narrative, and was coldly impersonal. In fact, his chilliness puts off the modern reader. Only when describing the lush tropical scenery of Nicaragua does he display any warmth, any feeling.

The most notable aspect of *The War in Nicaragua* emerges in Walker's passion for the truth. Every fact in his book is completely accurate, and scholars use it, even today, in their studies of his campaigns. At no time does he rationalize or make excuses for his failures, and nowhere does he boast about or exaggerate his triumphs. Occasionally he shows faint traces of pride in the military valor of his subordinates, but even these references are restrained. He allows the reader to judge him by his own achievements or lack of them.

The writing itself is stiff and formal. Walker displays none of the fluidity and certainly none of the ironic humor that marked his editorials in the days when he had been a newspaperman. It is almost as though the book were written by a different person.

However, in spite of its general dullness of tone and lack of color, and of the author's failure to emerge as a personality, *The War in Nicaragua* became a best seller. It went through eleven printings, and more than 60,000 copies were sold, most of them in the South. The North, it seems, had lost interest in him.

By early 1860 Walker was solvent again. But his style of living remained unchanged. He lived in an inexpensive New Orleans rooming house, dressed like the proprietor of a small country store, and kept to a diet that consisted principally of bread, cheese, and cold meats. He became something of a recluse and usually brought his food home with him so he could eat his meals alone in his room.

In April, 1860, Walker went to Louisville, where he spent a little more than a month visiting his sister. She was proud of his success as an author, and the interlude was the last pleasant one he would ever know.

Early in May he returned to New Orleans and found Fayssoux waiting for him with a story that fired his imagination. It seemed that an English merchant who lived on the large island of Roatán in the Bay of Honduras had come to New Orleans in search of Walker, and in his absence had told his story to Fayssoux.

Years earlier Great Britain had taken possession of Roatán, but on July 1, 1860, she was transferring sovereignty to the Republic of Honduras in return for substantial commercial rights in that country. There was an English colony of considerable size on Roatán, and these people, who had no desire to become subjects of Honduras, had protested to London, but in vain. Now they were prepared to seize the island the moment Great Britain gave up sovereignty. Then they would declare their independence and, if necessary, go to war against Honduras in order to establish and maintain their own government. Having had no experience either in military affairs or self-government, they wanted William Walker to lead them.

Walker instantly revived his grand scheme. First, he would help the English settlers of Roatán. Then using the island as his base, he would form an alliance with former President Cabañas of Honduras, who was the leader of the Liberal party there and currently banned from politics. Together they would overthrow the dicta-

141

torship in Honduras, and Walker would have a solid base of operations. Thereafter he would recruit a new army of Americans and lead them into Nicaragua, where he would reestablish his own government.

Within days a group of Walker's loyal aides left for Roatán, traveling on a cargo ship, and he followed them at the end of May. He held a number of meetings with the English colonists of Roatán, and together they established a hidden supply base on a small nearby island, Cozumel. Walker also sent a message to Cabañas, who had gone to El Salvador seeking recruits for his own revolution.

Returning to the United States, Walker pushed forward with great speed. Thanks to the funds supplied by the English settlers of Roatán, he was able to purchase a small steamer, the *Taylor,* and to recruit one hundred men. By this time the federal authorities had lost interest in him, and in June he sailed from Mobile without incident, heading for Cozumel, where arms, ammunition, and supplies were being accumulated. At the age of thirty-six Walker had taken a new lease on life.

His plan had only one fault: the British authorities on Roatán had learned all about it. All of the several hundred English settlers on the island had known about the grand plan, and they were friends with British officials, who dined frequently at their homes. Some of the colonists had been unable to resist the temptation to talk.

Britain had no desire whatever to let William Walker disrupt their plan to transfer Roatán to the sovereignty of Honduras, and they certainly did not want the filibuster to disturb the peace of Central America again.

The British authorities went to the government of Honduras with the knowledge they had gleaned, and together they worked out a simple plan that could not fail. Instead of transferring Roatán to Honduran sovereignty on July 1, the ceremony would be postponed. Not even Walker would be insane enough to attack the island while the Union Jack still flew there.

This plan was followed. A Royal Navy sloop of war remained at anchor in the Roatán harbor, its guns ready for instant action, and a full battalion of British troops remained stationed on the island. Walker was forced to cool his heels in Cozumel.

His supplies began to run low and, even worse, a ship that supposedly was bringing him large supplies of arms and ammunition was badly overdue. He and his entire company went on board the *Taylor* and searched the seas in the area for the ship. Eventually his fears were confirmed. The British had seized the ship and confiscated its precious cargo.

Walker belatedly realized that he had been led into a trap from the outset, and he knew that if he again returned empty-handed to the United States, he would be subjected to such scorn that his reputation would be destroyed for all time and he would never again be able to mount another expedition.

Cabañas offered him his only slender hope. But his relations with the former President of Honduras were precarious. Four years earlier they had parted on less than cordial terms. Now, with no chance of establishing a solid base on Roatán, Cabañas had no valid reason to cooperate with Walker.

Searching for a way out of his dilemma, Walker concocted yet another scheme, an idea so unrealistic that it revealed his desperation. Nearby was one of the largest and most important of Honduran cities, the port of Trujillo, which was guarded by a large stone fortress. He proposed to capture the fort, reasoning that the

Hondurans were displaying the usual sloppiness of Central Americans in peacetime and had understaffed it. Then he would take the city itself, and thus have something concrete to offer Cabañas in return for his help and cooperation.

Walker outlined his scheme to his men. He was completely honest with them, explaining that this was their opportunity to avoid disgrace and certain ridicule at home. They voted unanimously in favor of his plan, which indicates that he had not lost his powers of persuasion.

His battle tactics were simple. A vanguard would draw the enemy fire, and after the garrison had wasted large quantities of ammunition, as he knew from experience the untrained Honduran conscripts so often did, the rest of the company would storm the ramparts. Six of the men volunteered to form the vanguard.

The plan was even more effective than Walker himself had dared to hope. Three members of the vanguard were killed instantly, and the others were wounded. With Walker himself in the lead, the attackers led a wild charge before the defenders could reload their ancient muskets, and the Hondurans fled. The entire engagement lasted no more than ten minutes.

Having taken possession of the fort, Walker sent detachments to capture the customhouse and various government buildings, all of which fell without opposition. It appeared that his gamble had succeeded, and Trujillo was his.

His first act was typical. He issued a proclamation in which he declared that he was not making war on the people of the city, that he had liberated them from dictatorship, and that his one aim was the restoration of a democratic government of their own choice. He took care to avoid antagonizing the people of Trujillo, and with good reason: he carried no supplies of his own, and was dependent on them for food.

In the same proclamation he declared the city a free port, a gesture intended to win the sympathy of Trujillo's powerful merchant class. What he had no way of knowing was that he had made a fatal mistake by occupying the customhouse.

Under the terms of a private agreement between Great Britain and Honduras, the customs taxes collected in Trujillo were handed over to the British every month to pay off an old debt. Supposedly the sum of $3,000 in cash was on hand prior to Walker's takeover. Whether this money was actually there, whether the evacuating Hondurans absconded with it, or whether some of Walker's men stole it has never been determined. It is even possible that no such cache actually existed, and was invented by the British as an excuse to intervene.

Walker, who knew nothing of the alleged $3,000 hoard, sent an emissary into the interior to find former President Cabañas and strike a bargain with him. Before the officer returned, a British frigate, the *Icarus*, appeared in the harbor, and her commander, Captain Norvel Salmon, sent Walker a message demanding the surrender of the American invaders and the payment of the $3,000 in customs receipts. This was the first Walker learned of the supposed funds.

He opened protracted negotiations with Captain Salmon, exchanging note after note while he stalled for time.

When his messenger returned, he was mortally wounded in a brawl with other soldiers before he could tell Walker the whereabouts of Cabañas, but he did manage to scribble down the approximate location of the Honduran revolutionaries, deep in the jungles, before he died.

The exchange of letters between Walker and the commander of the *Icarus* became increasingly unpleasant during the days that followed. Captain Salmon finally delivered an ultimatum. Seven hundred Honduran troops were gathered outside the city, he said, waiting to attack the Americans. He himself demanded Walker's immediate surrender and the repayment of the $3,000 allegedly taken from the customs house. In return he promised the safe return of all the Americans.

Walker was tired of compromise, and he resented the high-handed tone of Captain Salmon's letter. He had taken long chances, but so far he had succeeded , and he was prepared to take further risks. His early biographers argued that he knew certain death was the alternative to success, and that he preferred a martyr's end to another fiasco, but that is conjecture only.

Indicating to Salmon that he would reply within twenty-four hours, Walker spiked all of the fortress's cannon. Then, with his men laden with all the arms, ammunition, and food supplies they could carry, he led them out of the city in the dark of night and headed into the interior in an attempt to find the rebel force.

The Hondurans who waited in ambush for him attacked. The brief battle that followed was similar to many that Walker had experienced in Nicaragua, and his force of fewer than one hundred men badly defeated and routed a corps of seven hundred.

He pressed on, carrying his wounded with him, and for several days was aided by a tribe of Carib Indians, people who had been oppressed by the wealthy rulers of Honduras and who sympathized with the aims of the American who said he had come to liberate them.

On his own again, Walker continued to push through the tropical jungle. His supplies were exhausted, so he and his men lived on bananas and breadfruit they plucked from trees. They failed to take the precaution of boiling the drinking water they took from jungle streams, and many fell ill of dysentery and fever.

Walker did not dare halt to give his men a badly needed rest. He knew the Honduran government was pursuing him with all the troops it could muster, and his one hope of survival was to reach former President Cabañas before the enemy could overwhelm him.

He came to a river, and there fought another battle with Honduran troops, again winning. But this was his last gasp. He had no more ammunition, and at least half of his little force was too ill to march. Walker realized he had to give up the struggle.

The following day a flotilla of boats from the *Icarus* came up the river, with Captain Salmon himself in the lead craft. The officer demanded Walker's surrender, and the filibuster agreed, on the understanding that he was surrendering to a representative of Great Britain and not the government of Honduras.

The flotilla was paddled back down the river, with the prisoners on board, and when they reached *Icarus* the vessel sailed to Trujillo. There, on September 5, 1860, Walker learned the fate that was in store for him. His men would remain under British protection, and would be returned safely to the United States. He himself would be handed over to the government of Honduras, the transfer to take place that same day.

Walker was stunned, and before he was sent ashore he dictated a brief, angry protest to a reporter from the New York *Herald*.

During the next week, which he spent in Honduran

147

captivity, Walker made no complaint about his own treatment, which was abominable. His one concern was the safety of his followers.

At 8:00 A.M. on September 12 he was taken to the ruins of an old fortress on the outskirts of Trujillo. A large crowd of laughing Hondurans, who had been given a holiday for the occasion, followed the troops escorting him. Walker had been given no trial, but none was necessary. His fate was sealed.

Two priests administered the last rites, and Walker was directed to a place against a brick wall. He refused to be blindfolded, and declined to make a last statement. To the end he was calm and, above all, demonstrated great dignity.

The first of three volleys fired by the soldiers killed him, and he crumpled to the ground.

The Honduran government refused a request to return his body to the United States, and Captain Salmon gave his sword to the government of Nicaragua.

When word of Walker's death reached the United States his name appeared in headlines for the last time. Some newspapers condemned him and others praised him, but virtually all agreed that he had died a martyr, the only end that could have satisfied him.

A few weeks later Abraham Lincoln would be elected President of the United States, the South would secede, and the Civil War would break out. During that most tragic of American wars Walker would be completely forgotten.

His memory was not recalled until the 1890's, by which time he had become a curious figure, a sad swashbuckler who had performed romantic, illegal deeds during a period in American history when lawlessness had been condoned and even considered patriotic. No statue of Walker has ever been erected anywhere, but he himself would have said that none was necessary because his valiant deeds spoke for themselves.

Selected Bibliography

Allen, Merritt P., *William Walker, Filibuster*. New York, Harper & Brothers, 1932.

Bancroft, H. H., *History of Central America*. San Francisco, A. L. Bancroft & Co., 1887.

Carr, Albert Z., *The World and William Walker*. New York, Harper & Row Publishers, Inc., 1963.

Davis, Richard Harding, *Real Soldiers of Fortune*. New York, P. F. Collier & Son, 1906.

Doubleday, C. W., *Reminiscences of the Filibuster War in Nicaragua*. New York, G. P. Putnam's Sons, 1886.

Greene, Lawrence, *The Filibuster*. Indianapolis, Ind., The Bobbs-Merrill Co., 1937.

Jamison, J. C., *With Walker in Nicaragua*. Columbia, Mo., E. W. Stephens Publishing Co., 1909.

Montufar, L., *Walker en Centro America*. Guatemala, 1887, 2 vols.

Neumann, Alfred, *Strange Conquest*. New York, Ballantine Books, 1954.

Powell, E. A., *Gentleman Rovers*. New York, C. Scribner's Sons, 1913.

Roche, J. J., *The Story of the Filibusters*. London, T. F. Unwin, 1891.

Scroggs, W. O., *Filibusters and Financiers*. New York, Macmillan Co., 1916.

Walker, William, *The War in Nicaragua*. Mobile, Ala., S. H. Goetzel & Co., 1860.

Wells, William V., *Walker's Expedition to Nicaragua*. New York, Stringer & Townsend, 1856.

Index

151